Creating Lives of Impact
and Meaning on the
Road to the C-Suite

KELLOGG

Women

Copyright © 2018 Sally Blount

Published in the United States by
The Kellogg School of Management at Northwestern

ISBN 9780-692-99543-3

Library of Congress Control Number: 2018904986

Printed in the United States of America

Book Design by Patricia Frey

Editorial Support by Ilyce Glink and Think Glink Media

First Edition

Pivot Points® is a registered trademark.

WE THANK THESE DONORS WHOSE GENEROSITY MADE THE KELLOGG GLOBAL WOMEN'S SUMMIT AND THIS BOOK POSSIBLE

Alexandra Badger Airth '95

Carol Lavin Bernick

In memory of Mary Jane Blount, from her daughters, Susan and Sally '92

The Bullock Family

Edith Cooper '86

Ann M. Drake '84

Kathleen Gworek Elsesser '93

Ilene S. Gordon

The Holden Family

Ellen Jamison Kullman '83

Wendy M. Nelson '99

Diana L. Nelson '89

Patricia Riskind '97

Sheli Z. Rosenberg

The Sands Family

Keech Combe Shetty '06

Jennifer W. Steans '89

INSIDE

WELCOME
GLOBAL WOMEN'S SUMMIT
GLOBAL WOMEN'S SUMMIT
Northwestern Kellogg

LETTER
to our Community

This book represents four years of work undertaken by Kellogg between 2014 and 2018, up to and including our inaugural Global Women's Summit held in Evanston on May 8-9th.

Our goals in holding the Summit and assembling this book were three-fold:

- To celebrate the investments made and victories achieved since Kellogg first began admitting women to the then Northwestern Graduate School of Business in 1966.

- To mark the end of an era by recording and evaluating all that Kellogg women and their peers have (and have not) achieved over the last 50 years.

- To equip and inspire Kellogg alumnae to make more rapid and substantive career progress over the next decade.

Impact requires focus. So, we decided to focus this book and the Summit on the observation that Kellogg women and their peers continue to disproportionately disengage from the C-suite climb before reaching the top. Despite half a century of equalized access in education and the fact that women have represented 50 percent (or more) of graduates from the nation's best undergraduate programs for over 20 years, our country has made little progress in increasing female representation in the C-suite, especially in the CEO position. This persistent inequality led us to pause and reflect:

If men and women are leaving the best colleges at the same rates, how is it that the financial and hierarchical end states that women achieve are still so uneven?

As a follow-up to this statement, it's important to state right away, at the start of this book, that we recognize that the C-suite is not the final destination for all women – or men – who attend Kellogg, nor should it be. We at Kellogg pride ourselves on preparing leaders for all sectors, whether it be business, government, non-profits or education and all scales of impact.

However, it is our belief that through greater insight into the C-suite dilemma, we will gain understanding that can benefit all Kellogg leaders, regardless of gender or what paths they may choose to pursue after business school. And indeed, as this book documents, that has already been the case. Our early work on the pivot point model and the corresponding insights around executive growth are already shaping how we work with our students.

In late 2016, when we decided to hold our inaugural Women's Summit, I had not yet reached the decision that the 2018 academic year would be my last in office. As it has turned out, being the first female with the honor of holding the dean's job at a top-ranked business school, the timing could not have been more poignant. As thousands of Kellogg women gathered – at the Global Hub, virtually and in locations around the globe – to celebrate this important milestone for Kellogg, I felt so proud of our alma mater and its rich women's legacy. I am so excited about the horizons ahead.

Sally

Sally Blount '92

Dean, Kellogg School of Management

Michael L. Nemmers Professor of Strategy

May 28, 2018
Evanston, Illinois

What Did Kellogg Do for Me?

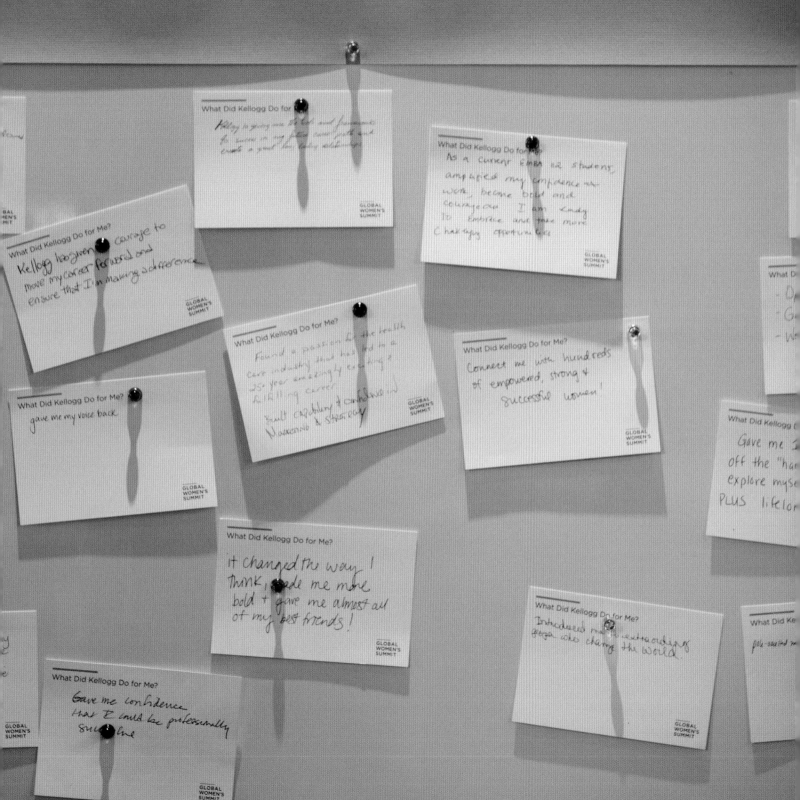

PREFACE

The Kellogg School of Management at Northwestern University has a 40-year history of launching female talent. Boasting more than 15,000 alumnae globally, Kellogg has been a "lead investor" among its peers in promoting the development of female leaders.

- Early glass ceiling breakers with Kellogg MBAs include the first female CEOs at Kraft Foods, True Value and DuPont; the female CEOs of major family businesses including Bigelow Tea, Carlson, Combe Incorporated and Lupin Pharmaceuticals; the youngest female chair at the NAACP and the first female CEOs of the Joyce and Weinberg Foundations, to name but a few.

- In 2002, a team of three faculty and alumni founded The Kellogg Center for Executive Women – the first center of its kind at a major business school. In the 16 years since its founding, it has helped prepare more than 1,100 women for the C-suite and boardroom.

- Also in 2002, Kellogg alumnae launched The Kellogg Executive Women's Network (KEWN) to nurture leadership, facilitate lifelong learning and build a strong and sustainable network for Kellogg women.

- In 2010, Kellogg became the first top-ranked global business school to appoint a female dean – a Kellogg alumna, no less.

- And in 2015, Kellogg welcomed its first class made up of more than 40 percent women, making it one of the top recruiters of female MBA candidates.

As we approach parity enrollments in our MBA classes, there is a need to take a fresh look at the issue of female talent and career development. We can no longer afford to assume that, in managing the pipeline of women into and out of excellent undergraduate and MBA programs, we have solved the problem. The numbers show that we haven't. In fact, despite these gains in education, data predicts that approximately 50 percent of the women who graduate from Kellogg and other top MBA programs between now and 2020 will exit the full-time U.S. workforce within 10 years of graduating, either because they choose to step out or are "forced out."[1] And many will struggle to re-enter the workforce 5 to 15 years later.

Spurred on by a catalyzing visit to the White House in April 2014, Kellogg made a public commitment to gain new insight and engage in a process of discovery. We engaged in small group discussions with alumnae and students, collected data, fleshed out a starting framework and hired a new team member to build out leadership programming for our female students.

We read articles and books. We reached out to leading organizations dedicated to female business leadership, including Catalyst and Women Corporate Directors, as well as leading consulting firms including Accenture, Bain, BCG, Deloitte, McKinsey, Mercer and PwC to share their learnings with us. We conducted in-depth interviews with 27 Kellogg alumnae from a cross section of industries, geographies, functions, ages and races. (See pages 173–187 for the full list and their short biographies.) And, working with a Kellogg faculty team, we conducted the first all-alumni survey, seeking insights on key questions about female career advancement from those on the front lines.

The first fruits of this work are outlined in the book you're holding, prepared as we convened our inaugural Global Women's Summit in May 2018. The Summit hosted nearly 1,000 women at our campus outside Chicago and reached thousands more through live-streaming and extension events around the world.

Through this book and the Summit, we've brought together research, data and real-world experiences to define and share key lessons and chart new pathways. In chapter one, we introduce our "pivot points" approach and growth framework for charting executive development across a career. In chapters two, three and four, we explore each pivot point in more detail and link them to the executive development needs for each phase. In chapter five, we share additional insights gained at our Global Women's Summit and in chapter six, we lay out a call to action for 2020 and beyond.

Our conclusion: this is an exciting time for women and for Kellogg. We are a leading business educator and thought leader. We have a unique culture and legacy of investing in high-potential women.

Through the women we have educated over the last 40 years, we have made significant contributions to creating greater gender equity. In the years to come, we will invest in female career development with even more attention and intention to catalyze more progress.

We believe that getting more women to the highest levels of business is important for our organizations, our economy, our country and our world.

Core development areas
People Management
Business Knowledge
Strategic Thinking
Relationship Building
THE EXECUTIVE TRANSITION
THE MID-CAREER MARATHON
THE LAUNCH
GLOBAL
WOMEN
SUMMIT
Northwestern
Kellogg

CHAPTER 1

PIVOT POINTS AND GROWTH

It is now well documented that the challenges faced by professional women are different than those faced by professional men, often in disadvantageous ways. These differences manifest in various forms, the most obvious being childbearing, the more nuanced being the unconscious bias that is revealed when women are evaluated as "bossy" or "aggressive" when they engage in what many would consider traditional male leadership behaviors. Or the fact that many companies are still surprised to find that they have statistically significant pay inequities between men and women that aren't explained by role or performance.[2] But these differences alone do not explain why, after 40 years of progress, women are still so scarce in the C-suite, especially in the CEO role.

In this book, we take a fresh look at the question: why do we lose so many

talented women on the way to the C-suite? To do this, we examine what happens to women as they graduate from college and head into the workforce. We study them across three career transitions, or pivot points. At each pivot point, we explore the different reasons women exit the full-time work force at higher rates than do their male peers.

Our starting hypothesis is that if we can find new and better ways to support women through three critical career pivot points, where gender differences come to the fore, we can keep more women in the workforce, filling the pipeline to the C-suite.

In the chapters that follow, we bring each pivot point to life and provide women with a deeper understanding of how best to build their careers over time. As we examine and integrate across the pivot points, we anchor our discussion in an executive growth framework. This framework highlights the core developmental lessons and experiences that need to be learned by all executives on the way to the C-suite. We start with the understanding that not all people have the intellectual, emotional and social capabilities or even desire to lead at the C-suite level. But for those who do, too few women get the opportunities and development they need throughout

their careers to reach these highest levels.

Getting the right executive development is particularly challenging for women because of well-documented cultural biases within organizations and motivational biases within women themselves (such as underconfidence and a tendency to accumulate less "relational capital" at work, relative to male peers) that affect how they

process and approach work. Getting the right executive development is also challenging because when women leave the workforce or work only part-time, they lose both momentum on the growth journey and access to opportunities they might have had for gaining critical experiences and knowledge.

Our second core hypothesis is that the best way to overcome the social and psychological biases that inhibit women's career development is to start with greater awareness from women themselves. Women in the pipeline need to get more savvy and intentional about their executive development.

In the subsequent chapters, we explore women's executive development by phase and through each pivot point. We use data and stories to offer insights, practical advice and inspiration for women seeking C-suite roles and for the men who support and mentor them.

The Pivot Points Approach

Before diving into the specific content, it's important to note that in this book, our focus is on college-educated women pursuing professional, white-collar careers in business. We narrow in to study how careers progress for the women interested in reaching the highest roles in business, namely the team reporting directly to a president or CEO (depending on how a company uses titles to indicate the highest role) and even the highest role itself. We don't expect or believe that all college-educated women do hold or should hold this goal. But for those who do, we want them to better understand the opportunities and challenges they'll face on this journey.

We conceptualize that a woman's professional career takes place in three phases, which occur in a predictable order. The exact length of each phase and the timing between them will vary depending on the specific woman and her family's unique circumstances. We are not implying a fixed formula. Instead, we are saying that there are three predictable constellations of issues that arise over the course of a professional woman's career, due to her unique biological and cultural standing in Western 21st-century life.

A work career begins with **The Launch**, which starts as a woman leaves college in her early twenties and extends into her early thirties. It's roughly a decade long. This is the period when women gain foundational work experiences and professional credentials. This is also when many women (and men) make personal commitments that shape how their later adult years play out.

The Mid-career Marathon begins sometime in the thirties. The timing can vary by woman, depending on when she achieves more substantive roles at work and when new personal commitments, most notably children, begin to make home life more complex. The key change is that work demands increase with more people and bigger projects to manage. At the same time, home life becomes more chaotic as babies are born, parents begin to cope with age-related illnesses and a partner's job becomes more demanding. Primary relationships are put under a lot of stress, which only gets heightened when new job offers, potential transfers and setbacks are encountered at work. This tends to be the most grueling period of a woman's

career and the period in which many women pull back from full-time work.

If a woman stays in the pipeline to senior leadership, **The Executive Transition** years begin sometime in the mid-forties to mid-fifties. The timing varies depending on the size of the company and when the woman transitions into a role that brings her into the C-suite. In this period, the woman gains significant work responsibilities. She "owns" the results for a big piece of a business or function. She is more visible and vulnerable in the workplace, as the competition at this level is fierce. But this is also often a time when personal commitments, while still complex, take on less daily urgency. Children are usually older and need less day-to-day attention, and some solutions have been navigated for aging parents.

As the above narrative makes clear, we take the view that professional business careers have a predictable cadence for women. That cadence shapes the flow and the opportunities that high-potential women encounter on the way to the C-suite. Below we elaborate on these three phases and then outline our executive-growth framework.

The Launch

Right from the start of their careers, today's female college graduates earn less than their male peers. This is true even at the most elite schools, such as Northwestern, Princeton and Harvard. Data from these institutions shows that, upon graduation from college, women earn on average about 80 to 90 percent of what their male peers earn, in part because of the roles and industries they choose.[3]

This placement data suggests that women graduating from these colleges are less likely to apply for some of the most prestigious and high-paying first jobs. A broad class of entry-level positions at consulting firms, financial institutions and Fortune 500 companies offer upward mobility for leaders across all sectors. But if women are not taking these jobs in equal numbers to men, even for a couple of years at the beginning of their careers, they are missing out on the financial and development benefits that these early career accelerators provide.

At least three factors appear to be driving this early disparity. First, young

women tend to hold more negative stereotypes about working in business than do young men. Second, women are still less likely to study mathematics, business and economics in college. Finally, young women still encounter relatively few female role models who can both demonstrate why working in business is a meaningful life choice and actively help those who decide to try.

A further manifestation of these gaps and misperceptions is the fact that business schools are the only professional graduate schools that

10 Reasons Women Fail to "Launch Well"

Most common reasons we heard:

1. Young women tend to have more negative stereotypes about business (e.g., the "bro culture" in tech, Wall Street machismo, consulting suitcase lifestyle, etc.), so many shy away from the most competitive business jobs or from business altogether.

2. Young women are more likely to prioritize comfort and fit over discomfort and growth, so they don't stretch as much at work as men.

3. College women tend to congregate in majors that lead to lower-paying career paths. Men are still more likely than women to major in business, finance, accounting, engineering or economics – all subjects linked to highly paid fields.

4. Young women tend to lack confidence. They often think, "I'm not qualified enough" or "I'm not good at numbers."

5. Young women are not always achievement-motivated in their 20s. Some think, "I'll want a better work/life balance soon, so why push now?"

6. Women are more comfortable negotiating and advocating for others than they are for themselves.

7. Women are less likely to make bold moves or take risks in early jobs.

8. Women are hindered by the likeability dilemma: having to choose between being perceived as likeable versus competent, because society says they can't be both.

9. Even before they are pregnant, women can be held back by the "pregnancy penalty." That happens when organizations don't offer women the highest-impact roles, because they fear they will get pregnant and leave, or at minimum slow down for children.

10. Women stall early on because they don't see role models "like them" whom they admire.

Source: Book interviews and 2017 All Aumni Survey.

still receive fewer than 50 percent of their applications from women.[4] This is true even though an MBA requires the least amount of time to complete, relative to other professional degrees, and can offer the highest potential for upward earnings mobility, especially for graduates of the most elite schools. Further, it has the most career flexibility. It can provide important grounding for careers in any sector: business, government or nonprofit.

The key insight here is that many capable women are opting out of business before they even graduate. Clearly, if we have any hope of getting more women into the C-suite and boardroom, we need to address young women's perceptions of business. We also need to change the dialogue among young women, especially those at our top colleges and graduate schools, about how to use their launch years in ways that maximize their chances for long-term career success.

The Mid-Career Marathon

The second critical pivot point occurs as women move into the mid-career years, when long-term relationships and caregiving roles become focal. For women who have launched well, the demands at work are growing just as the ones at home are. And while ambitious men face the same shift, research finds that in the U.S. – whether by choice, necessity or default – women typically pick up more of the burden for meeting their families' growing non-work needs during this phase.[5]

As the mid-career years progress, aging relatives get frailer and coordinating children's care and schedules outside the home get more complicated. Stress levels rise. At this point, many well-educated, career women – especially those paired with well-educated, employed spouses – make the calculation that it's just not worth it, economically or emotionally, to stay in the game.

The importance of this point was borne out more than a decade ago in a 2004 study of American women who left work to have children. Although 93 percent of these women wanted to return to work, just 74 percent managed to do so, and only 40 percent returned full time.[6] As current Organization for Economic Co-operation and Development (OECD) employment tables show, U.S. labor force participation by women aged 25 to 54 has not improved since 2004. In fact, participation peaked around 75 percent in 2000, but has fallen since then and now hovers around 70 percent. That is the same level it was at in the mid-1980s.[7]

It doesn't have to be this way. Denmark, Norway and Sweden – nations where high-quality, affordable child and elder care are the norm – all rank among the top in the OECD in female workforce participation.

There are also critical developmental needs for all high-potential professionals during this phase. This is a period when both men and women can lose career focus. They may make imperfect choices about what skills to build and what development opportunities to seek. These choices can sidetrack a promising career. But for women there is an added factor: the implicit and explicit bias so often present at work (in ways that many men still don't see) that just makes everything more frustrating and exhausting.

Research also shows that mid-career is the time when effective mentorship and sponsorship are critical, and conversely where the lack of good guidance increases the likelihood of a career exit for women. But workplace trends continue to reveal that women in this phase are less likely than male peers to ask for help and to pursue new opportunities.[8] Perhaps as a result, they are also less likely than men to find and be supported by strong sponsors.

The Executive Transition

For women who make it through The Launch and The Mid-career Marathon successfully, the final pivot point comes in the shift from running a piece of an organization to helping lead the whole. In the corporate world, this is what happens in the transition from, for example, a functional or geographic vice-president or senior vice-president to an executive vice-president.

Making The Executive Transition means broader scope, more responsibility, more meetings, more travel and yes, more politics. All of this translates into more time spent working and/or thinking about work as a woman navigates increasingly complex jobs, in more nuanced circles. The women who have survived The Mid-career Marathon have developed rich professional networks and support mechanisms. Yet, many of these women never make it into The Executive Transition, either by chance or choice.

The women who fall off by chance are the ones who get looked over (and over) when it comes to filling the C-suite jobs. Internally, people assess that they are not "a fit" or there is "something missing" when decisions are made. Externally,

no realistic alternative materializes that offers an opportunity for higher impact in a new organization. After a few months or years of sitting in C-suite limbo, these women either decide, or someone decides for them, that it is time to step out.

As for the women who opt out by choice, they do so because the potential benefit of the higher climb no longer seems worth the cost. Research finds that, in

The facts about women leaving the workforce

- By some estimates, 43 percent of highly trained professional women with children leave the workforce at some point in their careers.[9]

- Within two years of having a child, there is a 30 percent reduction in workforce participation among women with bachelor's degrees and a 19 percent drop for those with master's degrees.[10]

- For female MBAs, the story is starker, even if they graduated from an elite school. A Harvard study found that women MBAs have much lower workforce participation rates than their male peers.[11]

- A Vanderbilt study found that "the largest gap in labor market activity between graduates of both elite and less selective institutions is among MBAs."[12]

- According to a Harvard University study of business school graduates, female MBAs were 22 percent more likely than male MBAs to have experienced at least one career interruption.[13]

- At any given time, 13 percent of women aren't working, compared to one percent of men.[14]

Though more education helps keep talented U.S. women in the workforce, their workforce participation is still at rates much lower than those of their male peers in most First World countries.[15]

contrast to peer men, many women at this stage are not as motivated by achieving more money or a bigger title.[16] Anecdotal evidence from women who have exited at this stage highlights two factors: the temporal cost and the mental cost. The demands for face time and certain kinds of cultural interaction feel less rewarding relative to the monetary awards that might come with them. After making it so far, it can feel "ridiculous" to have to keep spending time in ways that do not create real value or impact, only the illusion of it. Further, this is the phase when, after years of confronting both explicit and implicit bias, the subtle messages and slights can become particularly galling.

Most women who make it this far in the business sector have earned good money and likely saved a fair amount. Each time something annoying happens at work, they report doing a mental calculation: how much longer do I put up with this? Numerous women we have met who are in the process of opting out in their early fifties relate some version of the following: "I've hit my number. I'm out. I'm going to join boards and start spending my time in ways that are more meaningful to me personally." They choose not to raise their hands for bigger jobs or even refuse to take the bigger roles when offered.

Note that men, too, must navigate this transition, but it appears that fewer men turn down a run at a bigger job. We hypothesize that they tend to set a higher "number" for retirement. They also are less likely, especially if Caucasian, to have been overlooked due to implicit bias. And given the preponderance of men in the C-suite of most major companies, they are also less likely to have to grapple with the emotional toll of being an "outsider" once they are on the team.

Moving into The Executive Transition phase requires a combination of motivation and opportunity. Keeping women in the game to the highest levels means beating the odds. Success here takes deeper intention on the part of both women and their organizations.

Our Growth Framework

As we examine each pivot point in more depth in the subsequent chapters and think more fully about how to support women through them, the goal is not to provide an exhaustive roadmap for developing C-suite executives. Instead, our goal is to make the developmental needs of each career phase explicit and to provide some integration across them. Broadly speaking, we focus on four types of learning, outlined below, that form the core of executive competencies, capabilities and experiences.

People management

Organizational leaders manage and lead people. Over the course of their careers, they need to master the basics of managing themselves and others, including managing upward, downward and sideways. They need to learn how to build and coach teams and to hire and develop talent, while also managing their own professional development and reputation with intention. Finally, they need to master the ability to help their companies envision or re-envision the future and to make that better future a reality.

Business knowledge

Business leaders need to understand the core functions required to operate a business, as well as gain some mastery in at least one of them. They also need to understand how markets work, in order to manage profits and product share growth in competitive market settings. Finally, they need to learn how to take an enterprise-level view that manages enterprise growth, margin improvements, risk and capital allocation over time.

Strategic thinking

Business leaders need to think strategically about how organizations and markets develop over time. They need to learn how to shape job, team and organizational structures, whether it be formal structures and reporting relationships or informal social networks, cultures and political dynamics. At a market level, they need to understand how to envision and enact inter-company mergers, acquisitions and spin-offs. At the highest levels, C-suite executives, whether they are line leaders or function heads, oversee organizational renewal and transformation as they strive to create long-term value, remake markets and even transform industries.

Relationship building

Business is all about connecting with people. Every organization is made up of people. Markets are made up of people, as are governments and nonprofits. Successful executives invest and build their relationships. They do this by nurturing an expanding web of substantive relationships over the course of their careers. The foundation of a network comes from staying in touch with college friends and expanding as connections are made at work, on weekends, at industry conferences and within a local business community. The web continues to grow over time, across geographies and industries, as do the interpersonal skills required to manage all of these relationships.

Conclusion

Women experience work and are perceived at work through distinct biological, psychological and cultural lenses. In this book, we take these differences as given. We adopt the perspective that the best first step in overcoming the biases, beliefs and norms that may impede social progress is through **greater attention and intention** on the part of women. In the process, we also look to educate the men who support them, lead their companies and sit on their boards.

In the pages that follow, we use the growth framework we've described to explore how these four types of executive knowledge need to be deepened and evolve over the course of a successful career. In the process, we outline the core developmental lessons and experiences that women need to gain as they aim for the C-suite. Our goal is to use the growth framework to sharpen both women's and men's understanding of the challenges and opportunities facing women in each phase.

THE LAUNCH

Careers unfold over a lifetime. Unexpected opportunities and obstacles arise – at work and at home – that affect how a career progresses, especially for women. The same job that may eventually lead one person into the C-suite may end in a stalled career for another. There are multiple paths and no guarantees. It's all part of the journey.

But we do know that choices made early in one's career set trajectories that increase or decrease the likelihood of long-term career success. A key question for gaining more gender equality in the C-suite is: how do we maximize the chances of success for our most promising young women as they start their careers?

Getting it "right" during the post-college decade can pay off for women in their thirties with faster promotions and better career options, leading to even bigger opportunities and financial rewards in their forties, fifties and beyond. Conversely, getting it "wrong" can have disproportionate costs over the course of a woman's working life, especially if such "wrongs" aren't righted in the subsequent decade. For women, the cost of a weak launch is higher than for their male peers, because the thirties are typically more challenging due to women's growing family responsibilities. That means there is less time and energy available to make up for a slow start.

The Four Cornerstones of a Successful Launch

While every successful C-suite career has a unique trajectory, the learning and experiences gained in The Launch stage form the foundation of that success. We can think of this work as laying the cornerstones upon which subsequent executive learning and experiences will be built and expanded. Significant gaps in any area can lead to uneven development and missed opportunities that can make the mid-career years more challenging, increasing the likelihood that a woman will pull out during that phase.

The good news is that the cornerstone lessons aren't complicated. In the modern workplace, the most important learnings of the early years will be around the phenomenon and experience of working in an organization and understanding how human organizations get things done. This means that as women leave college and hit the "real world," they need to shift from developing their IQ to developing their EQ and SQ – their emotional and social intelligences. To do this well, a woman needs a job in a functional and productive work environment. She also, personally, needs to focus on how to become a competent and effective professional.

People management

At the core, successful executives manage people well. The early lessons of people management include managing 1) your own performance, 2) your reporting relationship with your boss, 3) your performance as a team member and later 4) a small team. The post-college decade is the ideal time to gain these experiences.

Managing oneself well begins with self-presentation. It means adopting practices of getting to work on time, keeping one's work area tidy and organized and presenting oneself in way that looks neat and professional each day. All of these basics apply no matter where a woman works. Even if not everyone in your workplace behaves this way, it's what professionals on the way up do.

Related to self-presentation is one's work product, which must also be timely, well organized and tidy. When you hand something in, get it done on time, take the time to format and highlight key themes and takeaways, make sure that it is visually clean and sensible (not too dense or with too many bullets) and that it is typo-free. Or if it's an oral presentation, be sure to speak clearly, prepare and talk to only a few key points (ideally three, with five as the maximum). Minimize the use of words "like" and "um." As research finds, women can be disproportionately judged by how they speak.[17]

In managing reporting relationships, learning how to show respect and to deliver on realistic performance expectations is key. This means listening carefully when a supervisor speaks and holding oneself accountable for doing what you say you will, by the deadlines you have agreed to. If you can't meet them, anticipate that and let people know when they can anticipate your completed work. Supervisors don't expect perfection all the time, but professionals let people know *in advance* if they can't make a meeting or deliver a work product on time. They set realistic expectations.

"If you're talking, you're not listening. And if you're not listening, you're not learning."

Ellen Kullman '83

"Launch in finance. I've worked with many women who really weren't as comfortable talking about numbers. It's very limiting, because numbers tell a story. It's essential that whatever your career path is, you make numbers your strength."

Cindi Bigelow '86

"When I went into business, I went into sales. I think it's a great place for young people to start dealing with the customer, dealing with the product, really understanding the nature of competition."

Ellen Kullman '83

As team members, young professionals need to learn how to be accountable to their peers. Again, timeliness, reliability and respect for one's teammates and shared work products form the foundation. Peer accountability also means holding one's peers, and later one's own direct reports, accountable to high standards. And when a team member hits a snag, it is important to know when and how to chip in to assure that the team still achieves its goals.

Business knowledge

Successful executives gain mastery in understanding core business functions and processes and how they interconnect. The Launch is the time to master one function such as finance, accounting, sales or marketing, while simultaneously building a basic understanding of the other functions. This is the time to learn how the various functions connect through an organization's reporting structure and how other "connective tissue" (e.g., regular reports and meetings) drives decision-making, accountability and performance.

The best way to gain this knowledge is through conversation, reading and self-study. When a young professional meets people from other parts of a company, it is a great opportunity to ask questions about what they do and to listen carefully to how people answer and describe their work. Another important way to gain insight and knowledge is by reading the business pages in key national newspapers and subscribing to well-regarded business magazines. For those in support functions especially, (think HR, legal, corporate affairs), it may also mean reading up on the essentials of finance or marketing during off-hours, taking an online or night class in accounting or enrolling in an MBA program.

The Launch is also a good time to start tracking the business media on general economic and stock market trends. This stage is a good time to learn about unemployment rates, interest rates, international trade and the ever-evolving economic, social and political forces at play nationally and internationally.

Strategic thinking

Senior executives have a well-developed intuition for how organizations and markets work and change over time and how organizational cultures can both help and hinder performance and the change process. To the extent that a young professional can use the early career years to develop curiosity about organizational culture, politics (not just where decisions get made, but how) and competitive strategy, a career will progress more smoothly in the later years.

"In my first job at American Express, I was working for someone who was oblivious to the company culture and office politics. People around me were being promoted left and right, but not me. Finally, I had to get the courage to go to this man's office and say, 'Do you think I'm doing a good job?' He said, 'Yes.' 'Do you think I have what it takes to move up to the next level?' 'Absolutely.' 'Do you know that every other assistant manager has been promoted and that my not being promoted implies that I'm not capable?' He said 'No.' I was promoted three hours later."

Diana L. Nelson '89

"The constant thread for me is asking the question, 'Am I learning something new?' If you have a thread of intellectual curiosity, the rest will work itself out beautifully."

Anne Clarke Wolff '89

A great way to develop strategic insight is by studying reporting structures and job descriptions to examine how people design jobs and work processes at your firm. In most organizations, line roles such as sales and operations are typically accorded more status than are support roles, such as accounting, human resources and legal. This is because line roles produce revenue, while support roles are often seen as cost centers or "overhead." As a result, it's worth noting which roles and people report to the CEO and which do not. It's also meaningful to watch the language that is used and the processes that govern how meaningful decisions get made, announced and implemented. What management reports are regularly produced and what are they named? It's worth noting here that for those who aspire to reach the C-suite in a lead role within a support function (such as legal, finance or human capital), it is important to learn how to describe and tie what your function does back into the company's strategic agenda. You need to know how your function helps in making or saving the company money.

Reading a company's annual reports and 10ks – as well as those of key competitors – can support the strategic learning process. (It can also help you beef up core business knowledge at the same time.) Reading trade publications and online feeds about an industry is always informative. Observing how the language that people use in your organization compares to how competitors communicate can yield early insights as well.

Relationship building

Below the surface, business is all about connecting with people. Successful executives build their relationships and invest in relational currencies of respect, trust and fair-mindedness. They do this by nurturing an expanding web of substantive relationships over the course of their careers. That's what people call a network.

The Launch is the time to begin this task by keeping in touch with friends from college and getting to know new colleagues at work. Start with the people in your work cohort (people who started at the same time as you), your team and your overall department or function. Over time, the web expands as you start meeting friends of friends who work at other companies. By working, eating and socializing together, young professionals build a group of people at a similar career stage whom they can call on for help and advice as their careers progress.

"In business and life, success is not an individual pursuit. If one finds success, the building blocks will most certainly be filled with key relationships, people who championed you, joined you, advised you and worked with you. So start building relationships early and intentionally."

Wendy Nelson '99

"When you interview for a job, think: 'Do I actually want to sit next to this group of people for 12 hours a day?' Because they're going to become your family and if you don't find them interesting in the interview, you're certainly not going to want to spend all day next to them for the foreseeable future."

Anne Clarke Wolff '89

"If I could do it again, I'd be more curious and act on that curiosity. I would take the initiative to have deeper conversations with people."

Camiel J. Irving '14

"Succeeding at launch isn't about focusing on one topic or quality, it's about building the box of skills you need to allow you to handle different positions."

Efrat Peled '04

The key to relationship building is to be fundamentally curious about other people and why they do what they do. It is about asking questions and listening to stories, inviting people for drinks and meals, celebrating birthdays and sharing articles and books. It's about circling around regularly to check in. Successful relationship-building is also about being someone others can trust. It's never too early to start building your own reputation with intention. Regardless of your distinct personality, or strengths and weaknesses, being known for integrity and dependability, someone with whom others want to work and do business, is key.

Putting it all together

The Launch years are when the cornerstones of a career get established. Ideally, they involve mastering the tasks of managing yourself and your performance on teams,

acquiring core business knowledge, learning to think strategically and growing professional relationships. On the surface, the list is simple, but getting it all right simultaneously is not.

There are many distractions – the Internet, social media, dating, student loans, vacations, long work weeks, working out, roommates, parents, siblings and grandparents – not to mention issues of self-confidence, undeveloped communication skills and getting used to balancing competition and collaboration in the workplace.

The women who succeed in laying a strong foundation during The Launch overcome these distractions and build their capacity for self-discipline and focus. They stay even-keeled in the face of long hours and repetitive tasks, they observe and process how decisions get made around them and they make the time outside of work for reading about business and markets.

Early Career Accelerators

Finding the right work environment, where a young adult is given interesting work and regular feedback, and where she feels her contributions are valued, can make the difference between thriving and stalling during the early years. Note that this is not the phase for "finding one's bliss" or a tight "mission fit" at work – that's for later, when a woman has more experience, skills and self-insight. All that's needed in The Launch years are roles that expose you to sound business practices and a healthy respect for a company's products, culture and customers.

While many pathways can lead to the C-suite, there is a well-known set of jobs that offer some of the most reliable entry-level opportunities for a strong launch. We refer to them as "early career accelerators" and describe them briefly here.

Management consulting

The sheer diversity and magnitude of projects and people one is likely to encounter working for a consulting firm make this an excellent starting point for almost any career. Consulting can help a young professional progress in all four key development areas. Indeed, even two years in consulting early on can make an impact on a career. Just look at the list of alumni from these firms – they're leading organizations across all industries, sectors and geographies.

"Consulting provides phenomenal opportunities for women because you truly have the ability to shape your career into what you want it to be, provided you're doing good client work."

Wendy Woods '96

Finance/banking

Jobs that help solidify an understanding of the basics of finance and how and why certain projects get funded while others don't is time well spent. Being comfortable talking to banks and navigating income statements, budgets, cash flows and balance sheets is valuable for all future leaders. And the opportunities to engage with different kinds of clients across a variety of industries broadens perspectives and relational skills, as well as jumpstarting one's network.

Blue-chip corporations

While working for a blue-chip corporation won't likely provide the same breadth of exposure or hands-on experience that many consulting and finance pathways do, these companies offer some of the most reliable management training programs. Their programs are known for developing functional expertise, fostering organizational and strategic awareness and building key relationships. They provide a lower-travel environment and excellent professional development. Moreover, getting hired by one adds instant credibility to a resume.

"Venture capital can be great for women. There's only one measure for success: performance driven by what we have identified, invested and grown. That measure is both qualitative and quantitative. You can literally see that you are the person who led the investment, who led the decision to do this deal. If the deal does well, it's you."

Jenny Lee '01

"American Express was big enough and on the forefront of marketing and customer segmentation. They were really leaders and I felt like I could take what I had learned at Kellogg and immediately apply some of those tools at a place that was cutting edge on profitability marketing."

Diana L. Nelson '89

> "I really lucked out because being in a startup department, even though it was part of Northern Trust, I learned everything about business creation and the different elements of a business in my entry-level job. That has served me incredibly well."
>
> Jana Schreuder '83

Small businesses

One route less frequently talked about, but which we are bullish on based on our experiences and interviews, is the opportunity to work for a smaller, fast-growing company. As these organizations expand and move to put a basic functional structure in place, bright young 20-somethings often find that they can get hands-on experience in managing people, learning the basics of business and figuring out how and why decisions get made. These smaller firms may not yet have established management training programs, best-in-class policies and practices or even a full-time HR person, but many of the successful women we interviewed, as well as our own careers, suggest that the experience of seeing how all facets work together in a growth business can prove invaluable.

Business school

Another obvious career accelerator – not surprisingly, given our starting point was interviewing successful Kellogg alumnae – is attending a top business school. Benefits cited include a thorough understanding of business basics, excellent access to business thought leaders and CEOs, exposure to a broad array of organizations, early relationship building and extensive experiences in peer team management, all delivered in a relatively short period of time.

Despite the obvious advantages the jobs and schooling described above can provide, data tells us that many women shy away from applying for them. The general perception among young women is that these jobs are hyper competitive, requiring long hours and operating in tough work environments. At least from a distance, these types of organizations don't feel particularly motivating to women as long-term career options. When it comes to business school, some of the same perceptions, as well as the steep list price, can make that feel like a poor fit, too.

The reality is a little less daunting. Therefore the first lesson an ambitious young woman needs to learn is to not hesitate but to go for the biggest, boldest business job she can land in order to build her skills and credentials.

"When Kellogg came to Goldman Sachs and talked about what they had to offer, it really resonated with me. I loved that it was more creative, that there was a marketing element and a consumer trend element. It's all team-oriented. There were a lot of 'Ah ha!' moments. So when I left Kellogg and went back to work, I had more experience, more perspective under my belt and quite frankly more confidence."

Kathy Elsesser '93

Conclusion

The challenges of a good launch may be more acute for young women than young men. Anecdotal evidence suggests that young women tend to think more about comfort and fit versus building skills in the post-college years. Yet a tendency to over-focus on mission during The Launch can hamper strong skills development. Most people today don't land on their ultimate career path or organization in their twenties. So, young adults are best served by taking jobs in organizations that have expertise in developing talent during the post-college years.

Even for a person who aspires to a government or nonprofit career, business jobs can provide a strong launch experience. After all, leaders in all sectors need to understand how corporations work and the centrality of commerce to economic and societal wellbeing. Firms generate the profits and incomes that fund taxes and philanthropic giving. And because every organization can benefit from a basic understanding of management, finance and marketing, an early grounding in business can provide an excellent career launch for young women aspiring to lead in any type of organization.

The good news: there are many ways to gain business experience and accumulate the needed cornerstone knowledge in these early years. The tougher news is that some of the most reliable pathways require young women to engage in discomfort as they embrace paths they may not fully know, understand or appreciate, at least initially.

As our interviews make clear, investing the time and effort to take advantage of challenging business experiences and leverage well-known career accelerators will pay dividends down the road for

any woman, regardless of her long-term career aspirations. A better launch means better tools to use later in one's career – in any sector, at any operating scale.

KELLOGG  *Women*

How they made the most of their launch years

THEY MADE THE MOST OF INTERNSHIPS.

"I spent the summer before second year working with a Kellogg alum at his startup. It was a well-established business, but it was my first foray into managing technology, launching a product, setting the pricing, testing it, failing, doing it again. I'm so grateful I got that experience before I went into my second year and started building Brideside." SONALI LAMBA '12

THEY USED CAREER ACCELERATORS LIKE FINANCE AND BANKING.

"My plan was to become a lawyer. I went to business school as an add-on, actually. But when I got there I realized I could make a career out of it. I had always been enamored with numbers and what I loved most about business school was investment. I was intent on learning more about careers in investing, so I set about doing informational interviews with some of the largest banks in Chicago. I ended up talking with Continental Illinois, which at that time was still a preeminent national bank. At the end of the informational interview, I asked if there were summer internships available. The man who interviewed me looked at me and said something I'll never forget: 'We've never done it in the past, but it sounds like maybe we should consider doing it now.' And that's how I landed in the bond department on the Federal funds desk between my first and second years of business school. It was a fantastic experience. Fast forward and I had eight job offers coming out of business school, all of them from banks." PAULA B. PRETLOW '78

THEY CONNECTED.

"As I started thinking about business school, my mentors on the board of the nonprofit I worked at said, 'If you're so interested in marketing, you really need to start having coffee chats with folks in the industry.' So I identified 10 influential people in marketing who I wanted to meet. One of my mentors knew about five of them. He told me, 'I'm going to connect you to the first five. My expectation is that you impress them so much that they give you two or three more names and put you in touch.' That summer before business school, I talked to more than 100 people in the industry. By the time I arrived at Kellogg, I already had my narrow list of places I wanted to work and I had contacts at each of them." ASHLEIGH GIBSON '13

THEY FOUND GREAT ROLE MODELS.

"We have an unwritten family rule: if you're a family member, you have to have relevant work experience and an MBA before you can join the company. So my first job after graduating from Northwestern was with Estée Lauder, working for Jane Lauder on Clinique. She told me that she knew I was going to go back to my family business, but she wanted to give me this opportunity because she thought I had the skills and qualifications she needed, and because she wished someone had given her a similar opportunity. I appreciated getting to see Jane as a family member working in a family company that is public. Seeing how she used her voice in a way that was productive and business building, seeing firsthand how Jane measured what she said and how she said it was an incredible experience for me. I still think about that." KEECH COMBE SHETTY '06

THEY EXPERIMENTED TO LEARN WHERE THEY COULD THRIVE.

"When I started in consulting, I didn't say, 'I want to work in this industry or this function.' I said, 'I like solving challenging problems that matter. I'm eager to explore different industries and functions that let me do that.' And that's exactly what I got to do. In those first years at BCG I worked in telecommunications, steel, consumer goods and healthcare. For me, having the opportunity to experience something and learn what I enjoyed most was really important. From then on, my career has been about discovering the things I like most and doing more of those. That's how I've shaped it into something I love." WENDY WOODS '96

THEY WENT FOR GROWTH.

"Focus more on experience than the title starting out. When I left Kellogg, I was willing to do the ground-level work so long as that wasn't the only thing I was doing and so long as I was treated respectfully. Learning is like the interest you get from putting money in the bank early. I'd encourage more young women to be in the mode of learning versus the window dressing of titles, because ultimately they're going to be more successful if they are learning, stretching and growing, regardless of what their title is." BARBARA B. HULIT '91

THEY SAID "YES" TO STRETCH OPPORTUNITIES.

"From the time I was 7 years old, I had a goal to play professional tennis. So upon graduation from Northwestern, my next step was clear: I would follow my dream and obtain a world ranking. This decision delayed my more traditional career launch. But when the time came to launch my post-tennis career, I was armed with many valuable leadership lessons, but had limited marketable business-related experiences and no idea where to start. Then a door opened. My former tennis coach asked me to build a restaurant concept for him from the ground up. My first instinct was to tell him all the reasons why I wasn't the right person for this effort. He persisted and shared his belief in me. He said, 'You should have the confidence in yourself that I have in you.' He was right and my decision to say yes was indeed the perfect launch. That single experience introduced me to every aspect of business: market analysis, business planning and strategy development, talent attraction and retention, project management, financial analysis and management and capital raising and deployment. My takeaway was to never doubt my capacity and always say yes when offered opportunities that challenge me to develop and uncover new skills." WENDY NELSON '99

THEY TOOK RISKS.

"When I arrived at Northwestern, the man who ended up being my dissertation advisor happened to be running a conference for the Association for Consumer Research. We were having a get-to-know-you conversation and I mentioned a paper I'd done. He said, 'That's great! There's a session on that at this conference. I'll put you in the program!' I was thinking, 'You're kidding me.' But he wasn't. So a month into my tenure as a doctoral student I was presenting and got my findings published in the proceedings. It was terrifying but also empowering." ALICE M. TYBOUT '75

THEY GAINED EXPERIENCE IN CORE BUSINESS FUNCTIONS.

"My first job was in a product role. This role gave me the strong foundation required to work with clients on addressing their business needs. My job turned into a career when I began working with clients. I was interested in how human dynamics influenced decision-making and enjoyed the neverending learning curve of developing new client relationships. Sales was also a function where there was transparency and accountability. I set goals for myself and pushed myself to excel beyond them. The relationships that I built over the years proved to be an important component of my professional currency." EDITH COOPER '86

THEY FOUND WAYS TO ADD VALUE.

"I applied to Northern Trust three times and was rejected three times. I went back to the recruiter and said, 'I really want to work here. I'll do anything except accounting.' She looked at me with pity and said, 'I'm really sorry, but the only job I have left is in accounting.' And I said, 'OK, I'll go for it.' From day one, I was in survival mode. I had to very quickly appreciate the skill sets around me and figure out what I could contribute to make sure that collectively, we created success. I sat there my first few days until the middle of the night, trying to balance the accounts to the penny. I was not an accountant. Everyone around me was getting things done very, very quickly, but moaning and groaning about having to bind, copy and package reports. I didn't mind doing that and was good at it. So I said, 'Why don't we divide and conquer? I'll do all the binding and copying. You do the accounting.' And that's how I survived my first year. Then one day I got pulled into the manager's office. I thought I was going to be fired. But instead, this phenomenal woman said to me, 'We think you would be a great new business coordinator.' And a year later, I was in my first management role. I've been helping teams succeed ever since." JANA SCHREUDER '83

THEY JOINED NETWORKING GROUPS.

"I was introduced to a program called Management Leadership for Tomorrow. MLT is an organization whose mission is to diversify the C-suites in American companies. They look for young business professionals of diverse ethnicities and they assist them as they apply to business school and do career and passion planning. MLT was a game changer for me. Had I not joined this organization, I would have made very different choices about business school. I am connected to people from every major business school through MLT. I'm connected to companies I would never have had access to." CAMIEL J. IRVING '14

KELLOGG *Women*
Insights from the alumni survey

I think the key element of a successful launch is...

Lots of learning opportunities and broad exposure. Humbleness and thirst for knowledge. **Gaining expertise.** Analytical skills. **Strong training programs. Supportive manager.** Striving to learn as much as possible from peers, mentors and other sources. **Good networking opportunities.** Observing and listening, gathering a sense of how things work and don't work and what could be done better. **Opportunities to grow and opportunities to fail productively.**

The things that helped me the most in landing my desired job post-graduation was...

My persistence. My job before business school. **My specialization in quantitative methods.** A spouse who was supportive of my career choice and a good summer internship. **My alumni network.** My prior work experience. **My MBA in both marketing and finance from an excellent school.** Leveraging past jobs and having enough experience to showcase my leadership.

If you could start your launch phase over, what would you change?

Get serious about career goals earlier. Be more willing at launch phase to listen and learn and spend less time trying to prove myself. **Focus on learning how to navigate politics earlier.** Take more risks. **Start with a finance title. Jump into sales.** Be more of a sponge, learning as much as I could from the first organization I worked for and network more, especially with women. **Work in a company with a formal training and networking program.**

"**Keep track of the things you learn.** Keep track in written form. At any given moment, you may not realize how much you've learned and how good you are off the top of your head. So keep track of your accomplishments and the skills you've learned. That will give you a body of evidence and a boost in confidence that you can take from one role to the next." CAMIEL J. IRVING '14

"I have trouble considering myself a risk-taker. But packing up, leaving home, going to New York City and taking a very unconventional path with a startup organization changed the trajectory of my career. **So be bold and take risks.**" ASHLEIGH GIBSON '13

"In moments when I am making a leap, **I just think about the fact that there's really not that much to lose**. And if I do fail, which happens in life, I pick myself up, remind myself of my skills, talents and past success and keep going." TARRA SHARP '13

"Don't just think about the next two years or the next five years. **Think about who you're going to be when you're 50, when you're 65. What's going to matter to you then and what should matter now?** Constantly evaluate that for yourself." SONALI LAMBA '12

"**Use the feedback from people who have said no to you.** Every time you're defeated or shot down, find a way to use that as fuel to motivate you the next day." NICOLE STAPLE '12

"**Aim high!** Aim as high as you possibly can and everything else will figure itself out. Don't sell yourself short in anticipation of what you might want to do later, because I guarantee you, the higher you get and the faster you get there, the faster you start making the rules and making it work for yourself."
KEECH COMBE SHETTY '06

"It's important for women to jump when the opportunity comes, but **don't wait for the perfect opportunity**. Have a long-term goal, but be flexible enough to find opportunities that maybe aren't perfect. If you focus on the long-term, you'll get there." **EFRAT PELED '04**

"**Sometimes the path from A to B is not a straight line.** You may have to go around curves, over mountains and under rivers, but as long as you know where B is, you can get there." **JENNY LEE '01**

Life is challenging. Life can be difficult. But if you're confident, courageous, **have faith and trust the process**, it will be rewarding." **ROSLYN M. BROCK '99**

"It's different now than in my father's and mother's world, where you climbed the corporate ladder, stayed at the same company and it all made perfect sense. Recognize **there are so many different ways to develop your career and have a fulfilling life**. Be flexible and open-minded." **LISA EARNHARDT '96**

"There is one really important thing to know for a successful launch: **it often comes down to your friends, relationships and network**. When I started at Kellogg, all I knew was that I wanted to make a transition from the public to the private sector. It was only through talking to my friends that I thought about consulting. Quite literally, I believe that I ended up at BCG because a friend in my section had worked there, encouraged me to apply and recommended me. Had it not been for that, I don't know if I would have ended up in consulting or at BCG, where I've now been happy for 22 years." **WENDY WOODS '96**

"I would say my launch was rough. In hindsight, **I wish I had more perspective in those first two years**." KATHY ELSESSER '93

"I never felt any less than a male. We come from a very conservative community in India. Most young women are pressured to get married early and have kids. I always felt the need to make a material difference to our family business, adding value and managing the pressures that come with a growing business. **It doesn't matter if you're a male or female, it's knowing what is important to you and believing you can do it.**" VINITA GUPTA '92

"**If you think about feedback as a gift, it's really useful.** I think my pace of learning back in the early days was double what it would've been if I hadn't invited feedback in and if I hadn't had the luck to be around mentors who were willing to tell me not only the good stuff, but also and more importantly, the bad stuff." BARBARA B. HULIT '91

"Your first job is the hardest job to get. Period. End of sentence. But **after your first job, you can evolve and change**. You're not meant to figure out your lifelong career in your first job." ANNE CLARKE WOLFF '89

"**Whatever you do, talk in your first meeting.** If you don't, the longer you wait, the more pressure you'll feel that you have to say something brilliant. Consider yourself a full citizen from day one. Don't hold yourself back." DIANA L. NELSON '89

"**Learn that it is not a weakness to ask for help.** I believe that is actually more of a strength than a weakness. Asking others for help acknowledges their abilities, which in turn helps to form real bonds. A sincere ask for help, along with sincere appreciation for that support, goes a long way in building lasting relationships." CINDI BIGELOW '86

"**Just say yes.** I've done it occasionally myself, where someone gives me a special opportunity and I question myself and whether I'm the best person for the role. Men don't say that. They say, 'Great!' Saying 'yes' to opportunities is what women need to do." ANN DRAKE '84

"I think it's nearly impossible to plan a career 10, let alone 20 years ahead. **A role you're in today or tomorrow may not seem to be on your ideal career path, but it can make you a better leader or a more competitive candidate** for future senior roles." SUZANNE BLAUG '83

"I found I did my best learning when I was out of my element, when I was into something where I had no background. **Open up your mind** and really understand the capability there before you chart your specific path." ELLEN KULLMAN '83

"I've always valued the Oscar Wilde quote, **'Be you, everyone else is taken.'** The 'be you' to me is that I can't lose my core, my integrity, my can-do spirit. The essence of who I am. But the style, absolutely you have to select what fits the purpose. If you're always holding onto your core, it makes it easier to adjust your style, because you're not feeling that in doing so, you're giving up who you are." JANA SCHREUDER '83

"From the beginning, **I had the courage to say what I thought**, even if it was to the head of the division. And I really focused on working on the things that would make a difference in driving the business." BETSY D. HOLDEN '82

CHAPTER 3

THE MID-CAREER MARATHON

For young women who launched well in their twenties, the career terrain gets rockier as they move past the post-college decade and into their mid-thirties. As work responsibilities increase, so do demands outside the office.

The shift to The Mid-career Marathon phase is marked by two major transitions. The first, at work, occurs when a professional moves from entry-level to middle management. This transition means broader people oversight and/or responsibility for bottom-line impact. The second, at home, occurs when a women's non-work focus expands from taking care of herself to embracing significant commitments to others. This can include a spouse or partner, children, aging parents and even pets. All of these relationships require significant time and energy.

It's one thing to manage a stretch work assignment when you're single, but when work and life commitments grow at the same time, late nights and long-distance travel become more problematic. That's the official start of The Mid-career Marathon, arguably the most intense period of a career. And for those who got a slow start and are still working through the developmental goals of The Launch, the pressure can feel even more intense as they watch fast-start friends and colleagues move ahead.

As the stresses of the mid-career years build, many women start to fantasize about a simpler life. They imagine being more present for their families and friends, as they perceive other women are or as their own mothers may have been. The ongoing stress means that the day the nanny quits, daycare closes

Why women drop out

Why are so many U.S. women leaving the full-time workforce? Here is some of what we heard:

Work isn't compelling enough. The prejudice that women will be more focused on family than on work runs in parallel to the thinking that women of childbearing age may become pregnant, at which point they'll quit work.[18] A 2016 study from Deloitte found that nearly half the women surveyed felt they were being overlooked for potential leadership positions. This creates a situation in which women aren't getting stimulating assignments or being promoted and rewarded in a way that compels them to stay in full-time work.

Exhaustion. U.S. women still typically pick up more than half the burden for meeting their families' needs, compared to their male counterparts. They effectively work two jobs each day, leaving them exhausted and often unable to feel good about either role.

Cultural norms. Unmet needs for caregiving or household management leave women with an unpalatable choice. Among working mothers, 41 percent say that being a parent has made it harder for them to advance in their career. Just 20 percent of working fathers say the same.[19] Unless counter-balanced by financial need, this pressure from home too often provides women with a socially acceptable way to opt out or step back. Quitting is a societally approved exit strategy for women to get out of jobs they are not enamored with. Whereas for men, stepping back or out is still questioned or even frowned upon.

Mom guilt. It could be a working mother being ignored by the full-time mothers on the playground or a school system organizing last-minute school functions during working hours. Regardless of the trigger, the fact is, if a woman is working full time, she's probably feeling some degree of guilt about it. And she's not alone. As one workforce consultant put it, "The biggest competition a company has for keeping women in the workforce is a 6-year-old child."

Source: Book interviews and 2017 All Aumni Survey.

early or an elderly parent lands in the hospital, a woman's reserve and her resolve to stay in the full-time workforce can melt. The result: some 40 to 50 percent of highly educated women drop out of the full-time workforce during this period.[20]

The appeal of managing less complexity is undeniable, especially if there is a partner whose job can cover the bills, and the long-term costs of dropping out are not salient in the moment. But the research shows that the costs are dear.[21] From a financial perspective alone, the loss of current wages and reduced retirement savings can become devastating in the event of an unexpected divorce or widowhood. And it's hard to regain momentum 5, 10 or even 15 years later, especially if the mid-career developmental work was never completed. So while many women successfully re-enter the full-time work force, they rarely resume their prior trajectories, let alone make it to the C-suite, especially if they quit work completely.[22]

"Mid-career for an academic is often defined by getting tenure. There's this huge push in that first six years where you keep your head down, write papers and have a very limited life. Some of my fellow doctoral students were married and had kids while they were in the program. I honestly couldn't imagine how they did it."

Alice M. Tybout '75

The financial cost of stepping out

Women pay a steep price financially for stepping out in order to be their families' primary caregivers.[23] Research showed 33 percent of working women decreased their work hours; 29 percent passed up a job promotion, training or assignment; 22 percent took a leave of absence; 20 percent switched from full-time to part-time employment; 16 percent quit their jobs; and 13 percent retired early.[24]

As of 2015, women caregivers had $40,000 less in their retirement funds and saw their paid work hours reduced by 41 percent.[25]

Women who are caregivers are also significantly less likely to receive a pension, and if they do, the value of that pension will be about half of what men receive. The total financial impact on individual female caregivers in terms of lost wages and Social Security benefits equals $324,044, and the loss is presumably higher for women with MBAs.[26]

It's not just women's long-term career prospects that suffer. Research finds that most highly educated women who step out report dissatisfaction with their choice in just a few years, or even months, after the fact. While full-time caregiving offers many rewards, these women often cite a lack of intellectual and social stimulation. They miss their paychecks, the presence of colleagues and adult camaraderie and the overt recognition and pride in a job well done at work.[27]

As for the guilt that women often hold about not being available enough for their children, it may not be warranted. A Harvard study by Kathleen L. McGinn '92 finds that children, both boys and girls, benefit from having a working mom. The study reports that daughters of working mothers earn up to 23 percent more than do the daughters of mothers who did not work. The sons of working mothers don't show differences in compensation, but they do show significantly higher contributions to household duties compared to those whose mothers didn't work – a difference of 16 hours compared to 8½, respectively.[28] This research suggests, and our interviews support, that staying in the workforce and moving up in one's

career can be positive and rewarding for women, their children and their families.

For those who stay in the workforce and progress toward the C-suite, what are the developmental goals of The Mid-career Marathon?

The Architecture of a Successful Mid-Career

In this phase, successful professionals build on the lessons learned during The Launch phase, strengthening their core management skills and business knowledge, while gaining defter insights and skillsets. Since no one can excel on all fronts at once, this period is all about gaining focus, prioritizing to make tradeoffs, managing your own energy and your team's performance.

People management

In the mid-career years, successful executives move from delivering on a well-specified work product to delivering on a set of higher-level performance goals. To do that, they need to build teams that can execute on a variety of work products on time and on budget. People management skills

gain depth and nuance as executives achieve clarity about their own strengths and weaknesses and learn to build teams around them.

Developmentally, the mid-career years are a time to gain clarity about how others perceive you at work and become intentional about how your reputation is crafted. This may be through words, actions and work product – even body language, mannerisms and attire. Ellen Kullman '83 refers to this as building "the book" on you. Every organization builds one, either formally or informally, as executives reach the mid-career years. It's important to understand this, to know what your "book" says, and if necessary, to start editing it.

"One of my early bosses at DuPont told me there was 'a book' on me: a base of belief about who I was as a person and as a leader. He told me I needed to know what it said, because it would follow me throughout my career. But you can't always directly ask about it. You've got to do a lot of listening. You've got to do a lot of learning. You have to have compatriots in the organization with whom you can share information. It matters because if you know the book on you, then you can understand what areas you need to develop, what strengths you need to utilize and you can make great progress in your career."

Ellen Kullman '83

"You have to toot your own horn a little bit sometimes, as uncomfortable as it is because if you don't, no one else is going to."

Keech Combe Shetty '06

"Follow what energizes you. Determine what you do best, then invest like hell in those things."

Camiel J. Irving '14

"Life is a neverending lesson. Pocket your experiences and use new knowledge to help guide your path to a place that combines your strengths, your passions, your values and your long-term goals."

Wendy Nelson '99

Building your "book." The first step is to name and claim your strengths, whether it is running the numbers, writing decks, public speaking, etc. Build your list, test it with others and claim it (in appropriate ways) as you work. At the same time, it's important to begin noticing patterns in the work situations, tasks and roles that energize you versus those that tax you. Just because you're good at something doesn't mean it should be part of your core. If something doesn't energize you, it should not be on the list of things you're gunning to do more of in your career. The most successful executives consciously move toward and invest in the situations in which they are most likely to excel and generate positive energy in the process.

This phase is also about brutal realism in naming and owning your weaknesses, assessing which are fixable and which aren't. As Kellogg professor Carter Cast writes in

his book *The Right and Wrong Stuff: How Brilliant Careers Are Made And Unmade*, "Many of us are closer to career derailment than we might think. The fact is that one-half to two-thirds of managers and leaders will experience career derailment. At some point, over half of us will get fired or demoted – or our careers will flatline."[29]

For example, Cast explains, a reputation as a self-starter that might have propelled you through The Launch phase could morph into micromanaging your team once you're promoted to a managerial role. Likewise, if you've failed to develop the ability to say "no" to coworkers early in your career, you'll find it more challenging to deliver on your workload as you advance and your responsibilities become more demanding.

The mid-career years are absolutely the time to identify and tackle any major personality issues – that is, habits of mind that affect how you interact with people and behave in groups that have the potential to limit your career progress.

Building teams and developing talent. Beyond your own development, the mid-career years are when aspiring C-suite executives learn how to build and coach performance in others. This happens both one-on-one and at the team level. This is the phase when ambitious business women grow more intentional and wiser in how they hire and develop individual talent and, when necessary, make the tough call to fire a person, even someone they like, if he or she doesn't work out. Executives in this phase also need to learn how to assess earlier than they have in the past when a team is working well and when it is not, and do what it takes to fix it. Fixes might include creating a new set of reporting metrics, scheduling a team retreat to address

"You need to look at yourself and take an honest inventory of your good and not so good. One of the first things to focus on is developing yourself into someone whom others want to learn from."

Cindi Bigelow '86

"Working internationally prepared me to be a far better leader than I would have been had I stayed in a headquarters role in the U.S. I'm more open-minded about things. I look at problems differently."

Suzanne Blaug '83

a vexing operating issue, furrowing out a culture buster or low performer or jumpstarting the performance of a talented individual who is not fulfilling her potential.

To affect these types of moves, executives learn to monitor and shape team dynamics carefully, coaching performance for people who are both similar *and* different from themselves. The best teams have diverse talent, people who can make up for a leader's and others' weaknesses and biases and bring unique skills and perspectives. The human tendency to prefer working with people "just like me" is a liability that strong performers need to outgrow during The Mid-career Marathon.

Advanced people skills in this phase include getting facile at performance evaluation and feedback; negotiating within and on behalf of your team through social influence, not rank; prioritizing and setting agendas for the team and individuals; and facilitating team meetings that move team alignment, creativity and problem-solving forward.

Business knowledge

The mid-career years are when aspiring senior executives learn to deliver on performance goals that support broader and more significant company agendas. The stakes get higher as they move from building teams grounded within a function or geography to building and leading teams that cross functions and markets. A senior middle manager may be charged with the profitability of a discrete piece of the company – be it a brand, product category or geography – depending on how an organization is structured. Alternatively, an executive could be tasked with

overseeing HR, IT, corporate affairs or risk management across a large swath of the company.

Learning how to effectively pull people together across core functions, multiple geographies and/or markets to build a consistently profitable business unit, high-performing business system or high-impact functional process is critical to completing The Mid-career Marathon well. As executives start managing more people, including people whose jobs they may never be able to fully understand or do themselves, many need to change their approach. The task becomes more about understanding and overseeing process and performance metrics and less about the specifics of the work product. Managing without content knowledge or expertise is a tough transition for many female executives to overcome, but it's a fact of life as one heads toward the C-suite.

Performance at this level will be expected not just for one or two cycles, but across multiple months, quarters and years. Some measure of longevity demonstrates that it isn't luck driving success, but the leader's ability to monitor and make adjustments as external market dynamics, internal priorities and team capabilities shift over time.

For this type of learning, the size of the business unit matters less than

"I spent time not just in marketing, but in sales. I was hesitant to go into sales at first but then once in the role, I quickly realized it was such a great way to learn the business and the technology in our field. It really helped me understand the customer inside and out."

Lisa Earnhardt '96

"Business today is global. Learning how to accommodate different languages and different learnings is extremely valuable."

Jenny Lee '01

the complexity. Learning to run a small but complicated business unit can teach as much, if not more, than running a larger, simpler one. The same is true for "support function" leaders who aspire to the C-suite. It is better to be assigned to oversee HR, corporate affairs or legal in a smaller, more complex business unit where your role is central to the unit's ongoing success, than in a larger, simpler one where your insights may not be as mission critical.

For those aspiring to the C-suite, especially in a line role, this is a good time to gain "commercial" experience if you don't already have it. What this means is spending time with customers (be they internal customers for support functions or external customers for line roles) to better understand their current needs and develop ideas and solutions to meet future needs. Delivering organic growth and high customer satisfaction is core to sustained performance.

As one moves deeper into the mid-career years, business integration is an important skillset, so having some experience in a merger or acquisition transaction and the process of putting two businesses together to deliver on synergies is a plus. The same is true for taking on other challenging, high-profile (and therefore high-risk) assignments, such as a turnaround, a major new product launch or a market entry into a country new to your company. It's not always critical to lead the effort. It's often enough to just be on the team making it happen, especially for those leading core support functions.

These more advanced assignments not only help differentiate a person's "book," they simultaneously demonstrate the ability to identify opportunities for impact, to structure solutions to address complex situations and to break big challenges into tractable pieces that teams can deliver on.

Strategic thinking

As important as business knowledge and know-how are, the higher one moves up in an organization, the more organizational dynamics and politics come into play. It's no longer enough to perform well on discrete tasks or to deliver through your business unit. As executives begin to regularly engage with peers outside their immediate team, geography and function, it's time to start tuning your political antennae.

While many women dislike "playing politics," it's important to reframe this thinking and understand that politics are a fact of life in all human organizations and communities. Be it formal or informal, when humans gather they create behavioral norms and status orderings almost as soon as they interact. The bigger the organization, the larger and more complicated the political landscape becomes.

There are two levers that a successful executive can work in learning to manage politically. One is the "hardware"

of an organization, at least the parts that she can control – that is, how she designs roles, responsibilities, teams, reporting relationships, information systems and metrics to deliver performance within her area of responsibility. The other is the "software" of an organization. That means the working relationships, informal social networks, coalitions and overarching political dynamics.

The hardware is important because structural uncertainty heightens politics. Less defined structures tend to distort accountabilities, which can lead to a lack of clarity about who is responsible for what. Under weak leaders, organizational boundaries between jobs, responsibilities across people and teams, and accountabilities for performance start to blur. "Turf" becomes less fixed, even negotiable. Unproductive "finger pointing" flares when things go wrong. Such situations favor opportunistic subordinates, people who are drawn to building personal power and treating shared interests as secondary.

It is for this reason that leaders need to learn in the mid-career years how to build strong organizational structures. They need to master how to specify, systematize and measure performance. It is important to build structures that hold specific people accountable to specific outcomes. These structures matter not only to performance management within your area of responsibility, but also, as we noted earlier, for minimizing political dysfunction. In this sense, designing an effective organization is as much about assuring performance as it is about keeping politics in check.

When possible, a vigilant executive will also work to shape the organization at her boundaries; that is, where her responsibilities begin to blend with those of her peer executives. Metaphorically, one can think of this as finessing how your "processing unit interfaces with other processing units." This is achieved,

for example, by advocating for a standing cross-functional team that is held accountable for monitoring and improving performance in an area of shared responsibility at risk of "falling between the cracks" – and may be prone to blaming and factionalism across boundaries as a result. It might also be achieved by agreeing with a peer to sponsor a one-time task force to solve a long-standing, seemingly intractable problem, such as an issue with shared distribution or a supplier.

In general, the goal is *not* to become "a player" in organizational politics. Trying to play politics can be a dangerous and potentially career-limiting move in the middle of an organization. Frankly, you don't have enough structural power to minimize or protect against losing in a showdown with a peer or someone above you. Also, you don't want to develop a reputation in your mid-career as a "game player." Good people will begin to steer away from working with you, before they even meet you, with that type of reputation. The goal during The Mid-career Marathon is to build a reputation as a collaborator and honest broker who delivers.

Relationship building

This is the phase to build strong connectivity with peers, subordinates and senior colleagues, and if possible, forge a handful of deep relationships based on mutual trust. This is the period when you solidify who your peer allies are, and start tracking and sponsoring a small group of high-performing subordinates who have worked with you and show promise. This is also when you continue to assess and invest wisely in your upward relationships, being as open-minded as possible and not picking sides unnecessarily.

Finally, The Mid-career Marathon years are the time to start building connectivity outside your home organization. As a professional heading into her forties, it's important to build relationships across your industry and even other industries. It is also time to access a broader set of perspectives and insights through expanded reading, executive education

opportunities, association dinners and conferences. This growing perspective has at least four advantages. It:

- Gives you access to broader information and advice networks that can enhance your own performance (and ideally, also provide a broader support network of women on the same journey);
- Provides visibility and access to new talent that you may want to hire into your organization;
- Fosters greater objectivity and strategic insight on how your firm is situated and perceived in the marketplace; and
- Opens new career connections for you, if you ever need to switch jobs.

Core to relationship building in the mid-career years are headhunters. This is the time when a woman should actively cultivate relationships with a select group of headhunters in her function, industry or geography. Even if one is not looking for a new job right now, being willing to listen and, when possible, recommend suitable candidates is important. This investment will build your credibility and currency for the future. As you help the headhunters succeed and other people advance through you, you will become someone to whom others will one day want to repay the favor.

Tackling the Mid-Career Speed Bumps and Roadblocks

Beyond the core development needs we've outlined, there are predictable questions that each woman needs to answer at mid-life for herself and her family if she is to thrive at work and at home. As the thirties progress and give way to the forties, predictable physical and emotional transitions produce inner needs and situational stressors that must be carefully monitored and managed in order to maintain career focus and momentum.

Physically, one's body is not as young as it once was. Stress and sleep deprivation can take their toll, whether they come from work challenges, crying babies or the financial pressures of making payments on a bigger house, while saving for college and retirement. If parents need financial help, that adds to the stress. At the same time, unmet

"Do less to accomplish more. My ability to do anything well is predicated on my ability to give it enough time, energy and focus. That doesn't happen unless I'm saying no to something else."

Wendy Woods '96

> "You can have it all. You absolutely can. You just can't have it all every day. Look at things on much longer timelines."
>
> Kathy Elsesser '93

emotional needs for those who haven't found the right mate, or who have perhaps found the wrong mate, and the stress that parenting brings into marriage all mount.

Below we outline five core identity and coping questions that become salient for women in the mid-career years. The sooner a woman and her partner, if she has one, can find and make peace with their answers to these questions, the sooner and more likely they will find navigating The Mid-career Marathon both tractable and rewarding.

At Work

Who do I want to be? The first step is clarity. Professionals who want to succeed at the highest levels need to make choices. They need to place their bets – on a function, an industry, a geography or even, though less frequently these days, on an organization. One can't oscillate between paths forever, and psychological research has long shown that setting challenging but achievable goals maximizes performance.

Women who are not sure who they want to become or what they want from work will have a harder time persevering when professional and personal challenges heat up. The sooner during the mid-career period that a professional woman gains clarity (and peace) about her ambitions and what stokes and fulfills her sense of purpose, the easier it will be to gain traction, make hard trade-offs and achieve significant professional progress.

Am I in the right job? To grow as a professional readying herself for the C-suite, a woman must invest her mid-career years well. This is true both in terms of the organization where a woman is employed and the people for and with whom she works. Brand names become less important, as evidence of meaningful responsibilities and accomplishments come to matter more. This is especially true if a woman has used her launch years well.

Key to being well situated during the mid-career years is finding an organization with a good cultural fit, where a woman feels alignment with the firm's purpose. In contrast to the post-college years, the mid-career years are the time when a woman can and should start to place more weight on achieving mission alignment at work. To lead well, an executive has to believe deeply in her organization. Ideally, it should also be an organization with a culture and programs that invest in developing its people and

"When we look at why women leave the bank, they don't quit to go home. They quit to go to an equal or better position at a competitor. Why do they do it? Often they'll say, 'I was never anyone's guy. I wasn't their person. No one was pulling me into that great deal, no one was giving me that brutal feedback I needed.'"

Anne Clarke Wolff '89

"My grandfather used to quote the saying, 'Find your passion and you will never work a day in your life.' My interpretation was that one doesn't have a work bucket that is separate from one's life. One needs to live authentically and choose an organization that enables one to live their values."

Wendy Nelson '99

reward executives who invest in others. The basic truth: when a woman feels that she fits in, is valued and believes in the purpose behind her work, success comes more readily. The right fit makes it easier for all executives to manage the stress of The Mid-career Marathon and rally through the toughest days, both at home and at work.

Am I getting the coaching I need? Our interviews indicate that the mid-career is the time when effective mentorship and sponsorship are critical. Conversely, a lack of good guidance increases the likelihood of a career stalling. This is true for both men and women, but research suggests that women are less likely than male peers to ask for help and pursue new connections for seeking advice.[30] Perhaps as a result, women are also less likely than men to find and be supported by strong sponsors, which makes it harder to get frank feedback and get picked for the right stretch assignments.

Independent of whether one uses the label of mentor, sponsor or simply supportive senior colleague, the key insight is that getting to the C-suite requires coaching, and being challenged to grow. This is especially true as one moves more deeply into the mid-career years and needs more nuanced development. Ambitious men and women in this phase need senior colleagues who will facilitate and monitor their progress.

Landing a work setting in which the company, culture and support network are all aligned requires focus, realism and a willingness to undertake the discomfort and effort required to find a new job, when necessary. If a woman decides she needs to switch jobs, she shouldn't rely on luck or an out-of-the-blue call from a headhunter. Thorough research and advance planning is key. A high-potential executive needs to be able to show intention behind resume transitions.

"You can only make it work if you have help and if you have a contingency plan. I never had live-in help, but I always had a primary person A who was willing to stay over and help if I needed it. And I also always had person B, C and D who could help out in a bind. Contingency planning is key to mitigating your risk."

Betsy D. Holden '82

"My grandfather used to say, 'The harder I work, the luckier I get.' And in my life, I have found this to be true."

Wendy Nelson '99

At home

Who's watching the kids? Whether part of a working couple or a single mother with children, you need to know who's watching the kids, what the back-up plan is and what will happen if childcare falls through. This is a classic speed bump for women during the mid-career years. And if there is a child with special needs, this may mean that the C-suite becomes an unrealistic goal. There's always some luck, as well as skill and hard work, in who makes it to the C-suite and who doesn't. For those who encounter higher than average hurdles at home, the C-suite may not be a realistic option. The good news is that there are many worthwhile avenues for talented women to pursue. There is *never* only one path to creating a life of impact and meaning.

Whose career comes first? In our experience, it is a rare couple in which both partners achieve the highest levels of career success. Typically women step back and let their husband's lead, but for many of the highest-performing women we interviewed, when she hit the career accelerator, her partner agreed to sacrifice on status and achievement in order to cover the home front. Part of preparing for success means having the tough conversations about whose career comes first, if you have to choose.

When a woman becomes the primary breadwinner, that doesn't mean she's got an easy road. For a marriage to thrive, our interviews reinforced that spouses and partners require and deserve significant time and emotional investment to feel enriched, valued and affirmed. In the words of Betsy D. Holden '82: "Marriage is a team sport. Whether your spouse works full time or steps back to play a more supportive role, it is so important that they feel respected and appreciated for the critical role they play. We always did sort of a rolling 5 year plan to figure out how to make things work for both our careers. I never would have made it to the C-suite without my husband's support." As the careers we explored make clear, a supportive partner helps advance women to the top. Conversely, a rocky home life can make getting to the C-suite an unmet dream.

"When my daughter was born, my husband had just turned 50. We looked at each other and said, this is so precious that one of us is staying home. Then he said, 'Don't even think about it. I'm going to be that one.' That was probably the underpinning of what made everything work."

Jana Schreuder '83

"After just a few dates, I started talking to my now husband about my career ambitions. I was very upfront with him that I was a strong, independent, career-focused woman who wanted to work. I raised it early because a lot of guys I came across were intimidated, which I found out later, and I didn't want a guy like that. He told me, 'I'm okay if your career moves faster than mine.' And that was that. We're still figuring out our careers together. But knowing he is supportive allows me to dream big."

Tarra Sharp '13

Expectations versus reality in dual income households

In a survey of more than 25,000 graduates of Harvard Business School, more than half the men whose age makes them a member of either Gen X or the Baby Boomers said that when they left HBS, they expected that their careers would take priority over their spouses' or partners'. And the reality has exceeded even their expectations. While 56 percent of Baby Boomers expected that sort of "traditional" arrangement, 74 percent got it. Somewhat surprisingly, 61 percent of Gen X men had that expectation (more than their older Boomer male cohort), and 70 percent reported their careers did in fact take priority over their spouses' or partners'.[31]

By contrast, while the vast majority of their female counterparts said they anticipated their careers would take equal priority with those of their spouse or partner, a full 40 percent reported that in reality their lives followed the traditional pattern, with their spouses' or partners' jobs taking priority.[32] (Notably, these outcomes vary when the racial makeup of graduates is taken into account, with Black women as the least likely cohort to have their partners' careers take precedence.)

Related to this finding that women's careers often end up being subordinate to their partners', it is not surprising that on average, 54 percent of women surveyed said they do all or most of the household work compared to just 22 percent of men.[33] This suggests that even when equality at work and at home is anticipated, it is all too often not achieved.

Conclusion

If we are going to get more women into the C-suite and other significant leadership positions, we need more women to stay in the full-time workforce on pace with their male peers during The Mid-career Marathon. While it's never easy, our interviews make clear that if a woman can gain clarity on what she is trying to achieve; find the right organization, role and support relationships; and resolve the hard questions about herself and her home life, the odds begin to move in her favor.

KELLOGG Women

How they survived and thrived
the mid-career marathon

THEY PUT ASIDE SELF-DOUBT.

"I was offered the chance to be the head of national sales for a division of my company. I remember distinctly asking, when I was offered the job, 'Really? You think I'm ready for that? You really think I'm qualified?' I was in such a fortunate position because the leader who had made that offer set me straight in a few words, saying, 'Lisa, I never want to hear you say that ever again.' Sometimes we create our own roadblocks as women. A male counterpart likely would never have said the same thing. He would have said, 'Absolutely! I'm in!'" LISA EARNHARDT '96

THEY FOUND THEIR OWN STYLE.

"I was fortunate to have several women role models early in my career. One was a nurse who had been a state health director in the Midwest for many years. She taught me about board politics and how I should develop my own style of leadership. I watched how she led board strategy meetings and would try in these very formal settings to emulate her style when it was my turn to make a report. After a few meetings, she pulled me aside and said, 'Roslyn, you can't be me. Be you.' Lesson learned. Be your authentic self." ROSLYN M. BROCK '99

THEY LEARNED THEIR STRENGTHS AND WEAKNESSES.

"I started my career as a high school English teacher, and then transitioned into interior design before taking over my father's company. So I had useful experiences in creating a vision and mobilizing people to get there together. But I also had a lot to learn. So I surrounded myself with people who had complementary skills and knowledge. I'm still not good at a lot of the technical aspects, but we have accountants and lawyers and operations people who are really good at those things. For me, it's always about connecting the dots – what do you see here that connects there? That's my unique contribution." ANN DRAKE '84

THEY DEALT WITH THE SECOND SHIFT.

"As good and as wonderful as my husband is, he's no wife. I mean that in a gender-neutral way. My fellow partners who were male would go home and their dinner would be made, their house would be taken care of, their dry cleaning would be in the closet. As much help as you put around you, there's just a ton of obligations that our society today still delegates to women and mothers. If the kids get a hangnail at school, the nurse still calls me, even though she knows that my husband stays home. Those types of things made it so much harder for me than for my male counterparts, and the lack of recognition by the leadership regarding these types of things was so painful at times." KATHY ELSESSER '93

THEY FOUND ADVOCATES.

"Within organizations, people are often very focused on getting a sponsor or mentor. I think finding an advocate is really important. I try to connect with individuals whom I look up to and spend time picking their brains and learning. It doesn't even have to be a formal arrangement. When I approach them, I try to keep it super short, so it doesn't feel like a major time investment – 15 to 20 minutes maximum. People always like talking about themselves and the things they've accomplished, so I often focus initial conversations on them. What I've found is that once you start developing these relationships, when those people need help or have opportunities, they often think of you and they trust you to get the job done." ASHLEIGH GIBSON '13

THEY LED THEIR COMPANIES INTO NEW MARKETS.

"As Lupin was preparing to get into the U.S. market with a generic drug, the U.S. branded version of that drug disappeared. I said to myself, 'If you don't have a brand, how do you launch a generic, as a generic basically takes share from a brand?' We did some market research and realized the physicians really valued the drug. So even though we weren't in the brand business, I thought we had a unique opportunity to license the trademark and launch this product as a brand in the U.S. I convinced our leadership team that this was a rare opportunity – the market was established, the physicians valued the product and brand and we were the only ones with the product with virtual exclusivity. So, we seized the opportunity and actually launched Lupin in the U.S. on the back of this branded product." VINITA GUPTA '92

THEY HONED THEIR PEOPLE MANAGEMENT SKILLS.

"When I moved into the frozen pizza division at Kraft, the exiting president said, 'You know, this is a man's business.' To which I said, 'There are some things I can change, but that's not one of them.' I talked to each person on my new team to understand their issues. I found out that this was a group of men who had built this business from a very small base and had really bonded. They not only worked together, they fished together, they golfed together, they hunted together. And they were afraid I was going to ruin that. I said to them, 'I will golf with you, I will fish with you but you guys have to spa with me.' It ended up being a fabulous run for all of us. I learned a lot about transitions, and talking to people and understanding how they're feeling, what their issues are, what their hopes and dreams are, what their fears are, then working through them in an open and transparent way." BETSY D. HOLDEN '82

THEY HAD GOOD CHILDCARE.

"I was a single mom for a few years. When my daughter was almost four, she started at the day care facility here at the Harvard Business School. It was really great being able to drive to work and bring her with me. The woman who ran the program at the time taught me so much about how to be a good mom. Having excellent childcare providers in my life and in my daughter's life has been a gift." KATHLEEN L. MCGINN '92

THEY OVERCAME MOM GUILT.

"When my son was young, I was typically out of the house before he got up. But on the days that I wasn't, it was really hard, because he didn't want me to leave. One day I said, 'Eddie, I've got to go. I have to get to work.' And he said, 'Why do you have to go to work?' I started off saying what working parents often do about how I work so we can pay for the house and go on vacation, etc. Then I stopped myself mid-sentence and said, 'You know what? I go to work because it makes me happy.' After that day, he's never asked me again. Because what kid doesn't want their mom to be happy?" BARBARA B. HULIT '91

THEY SURROUNDED THEMSELVES WITH SUPPORTIVE WOMEN.

"I think it's unacceptable for a woman to feel like a failure. I know I felt like I never did anything well. Was I doing my job well enough? Was I taking care of the kids and the house well enough? My husband and I, was our relationship strong enough? You just feel like you're not 100 percent at anything. But I had a group of good female friends. Some were stay-at-home moms, some ran small companies or worked in big companies. What we realized was that you had to do what you were good at and then you had to get help with the rest." ELLEN KULLMAN '83

THEY PRIORITIZED AND MADE TRADEOFFS.

"My path has always been, 'How do I make what I'm doing more manageable?' as opposed to 'How do I stop?' There's always the potential to get overwhelmed with what you're doing. When you're doing something you love, I think it's much more about the choices we make, being willing to prioritize and finding the degrees of flexibility that do exist, to make it more manageable, rather than stopping." WENDY WOODS '96

KELLOGG Women
Insights from the alumni survey

If you could start the mid-career phase over, what would you do differently?

Take a more long-term perspective to weather rocky periods. Set up my career in a way to better accommodate the demands of child-rearing, so I could stay in. **Negotiate harder for promotions/raises earlier.** Take less time off to stay home with small children (I took 10 years). I was willing to go back part-time, but couldn't find any positions. **Work harder to integrate family and career.** Set better boundaries around work during personal time (evenings, weekends, vacations). **Work harder to find the right sponsors to discuss my career development and opportunities.** Switch out of my first job earlier – now that I am having kids, it is much more challenging to balance professional aspirations and growth opportunities. **Increase my awareness of office politics and be a better politician.** Be more strategic about it early on – in other words, figure out where and what I wanted to do and pursue that from the start – mid-career changes are difficult. **Take time for more lateral moves that strengthened my breadth of experience.** Not pin my career so closely to that of my boss, despite the fact he was an important sponsor. I would not have opted out mentally when things got really difficult politically. I would have sought different mentors to help me build a tougher skin without losing my values. Learn how to have more balance and flexibility in my life earlier, before it created health and family issues. **I'm not a "would've, could've, should've" person, but I think everyone, and especially women, could benefit from a strong support network, a solid understanding of negotiating skills and more mentoring/sponsorship.** Left my longtime job earlier to pursue work that made me happier. I let fear, money and a certain degree of comfort override my better judgment. **Spend more time considering the correct career path for my skill set.**

KELLOGG *Women*

Last word on The Mid-Career Marathon

"As a woman moves into the part of her career that puts significant demands on both her family and career, **I believe flexible scheduling is extremely helpful in creating a better balance**. It requires a tremendous amount of discipline, which I think women excel at. Pushing that request with a leadership team is something I believe a woman can definitely do now more than ever." CINDI BIGELOW '86

"There have been several times in my career when I had to make a choice between my job and personal relationships. I had to ask myself, 'Should I move to be with a man or should I take a leap and move to New Zealand for an exciting job?' **Many times, I decided it was more exciting to travel and further my career.** I think it's important that women realize that this is a valid choice, if it's what they want." SUZANNE BLAUG '83

"**Make time for self-care.** Identify what makes you come alive and the things that center and ground you. These are critical touchstones that will help you move forward when challenges arise. Your journey to success may not be my journey – it's important to affirm each other in our own unique career paths. Whether you decide to get married and have children or stay single and travel the world, do what's best for you." ROSLYN M. BROCK '99

"I jokingly say that women have to stay in the game and keep working because when your kids are teenagers they stop listening to you, but people at work still listen. **Having the company of other adults helps you keep the balance as your children become more and more independent.** Think about being at home without a community of other interesting professionals. Imagine how lonely that could be." ANNE CLARKE WOLFF '89

"**I don't believe anyone who says they make it all work perfectly,** because that's not possible. You just have to keep putting one foot in front of the other. It's very much about preparing for a moment, living in that moment and putting your best foot forward in that moment. That, and not being afraid to ask for help." KEECH COMBE SHETTY '06

"My first ten years were very difficult. There was a lot of frustration, self-doubt and occasional tears. Thank God for my women's networks! **The most important thing a woman can do is get involved with a handful of networks.** The women I met then are still some of my very best friends. That group really surrounded me with what I needed and supported me when I called." ANN DRAKE '84

"I've learned to **relentlessly outsource** things that I don't want to do, whether it be grocery shopping, laundry or dry cleaning. That way, when I'm home, I'm doing things I enjoy with my husband and son." LISA EARNHARDT '96

"Always have an agenda and play a ground game. Men have an agenda. They'll move the ball down the field five yards, get pushed back two, they don't care. They just keep playing the ground game, moving the ball up the field. Women, in my opinion, tend to hold the ball really tightly and look for the great pass. Before you know it, they throw the ball all the way down the field and sure enough it's caught. Both ways get you a touchdown, but you didn't generate any confidence along the way if you held all the responsibility and threw a Hail Mary. The guy that plays the ground game, he got people to understand his moves and his philosophy along the way, so in addition to scoring the touchdown, his credibility is now much higher. **Women need the confidence to rely on others and realize they don't have to do it all by themselves.**" KATHY ELSESSER '93

"As business leaders we tend to look beyond the present and focus on either planning for the future or analyzing the past. When my son was born, I was in a critical phase of evolution of our team in the U.S. I was initially overwhelmed with the demands both at work and at home. I learned to adapt to **make the most of the present**. As I look back, I am grateful to have enjoyed every moment both at work and home throughout that time." VINITA GUPTA '92

"**Be willing to take feedback and actively seek it out.** Everybody has developmental needs, so you shouldn't be upset that you have them. You just need to work on them. The fact that nobody's talking to you about them doesn't mean they're not there. It just means you're in the dark." BARBARA B. HULIT '91

"You will expend less mental energy and have more brain space to do your job and create value if you're not constantly trying to make people comfortable by not being you. You can **find strength and find competitive advantage in focusing on the fabric of who you are** versus trying to be like other people." CAMIEL J. IRVING '14

"There will be disagreement. There will be annoyances with the people you work with. But at the end of the day you should **always give respect, demand respect in return** and know when to walk away." SONALI LAMBA '12

A lot of times it's just about giving yourself the opportunity to take that first step and then make it work. **In every career change, I've never known if I was going to make it, but I knew I was going to try very hard to make sure I gave myself a good chance of succeeding.**" JENNY LEE '01

"There's a much more multi-faceted chess game you have to play if you want to have other important dimensions in life, particularly kids. There are times when you can say, 'I can get through a really tough year or so.' But to sign up for something that puts you in a conflict position for a really long period is untenable for most people. **You have to be really honest with yourself about your boundaries.**" DIANA L. NELSON '89

"**I believe in sharing your career with your children.** I don't believe in having it separate. So if I travel a lot, I sometimes take my partner and/or my children with me. When they come with you to work, they really understand what you do. It can be hugely beneficial for children. To be honest, they can often learn much more than they do in school." EFRAT PELED '04

"The problem is that we doubt ourselves. We're uncomfortable taking risks. The odds are for success. And even if it's not the kind of success you thought, **you'll learn from those things that don't go the way you had planned.** They make you stronger for the next round." PAULA B. PRETLOW '78

"**It's not about balance, it's about harmony.** It's about everybody you care about in your life, whether that's your partner, children, parents, friends or your team, feeling a part of your tradeoff decisions and knowing you're present for them when it matters most." JANA SCHREUDER '83

"**For me, one of the biggest learnings was about self-care and being in the right headspace to bring energy and inspiration to the business every day.** I wake up in the morning and think: Is this still fun? Am I still grateful for this job? Do I still want to go to work? If yes, I keep going. If I were really questioning that, I might choose a different path." NICOLE STAPLE '12

"Many women come into roles, put their heads down and just do the job. I've definitely had situations like that where I focused solely on the work and got overlooked for a promotion. You have to **learn to look beyond your daily tasks and to be an advocate for yourself**." TARRA SHARP '13

"In my professional life, I'm not great at delegating or finding the right people to help me. That's not a strength of mine. But in my personal life, **hiring help is a necessity**. If you're having a serious career, you're not weeding the garden or cleaning the house." ALICE M. TYBOUT '75

"Mid-career can be a challenging time for all women, whether you're single, just starting families or raising children. When you're single and in a demanding career, meeting people takes a big effort. But **you have to make the space for the relationships that can feed you in ways your career can't**." WENDY WOODS '96

CHAPTER 4

THE EXECUTIVE TRANSITION

We began chapter two with the observation that careers unfold over time. As our many stories reveal, the unfolding is a long process, especially for women who take on the demands of balancing full personal and professional lives. For women still in the game in their late forties, the altitude changes. These executives now oversee a substantial piece of business or a function and are leveraged by teams of dozens, hundreds and even thousands of people who are responsible for delivering the results that they "own." The C-suite – the opportunity to report directly to the CEO or president and, perhaps eventually, to move into the top spot – is now in view.

The challenge at this stage is that many of these women are tired. They have faced significant career and life challenges over the last 20+ years.

They have forged a journey that has yielded many wins, but likely also some bruises and hard lessons. As children and parents grow older, these highly accomplished women often start to reflect on what they have achieved and what life goals they still want to pursue. The result is that, with more frequency than feminists may like to admit, many women step out at this pivot point – just before gaining access to the C-suite – despite how far they've come.

For some, it's an issue of sustaining motivation after decades of powering through. For others, the nod never comes. They get blocked by implicit or even explicit bias, or the right opportunity doesn't open up at the right time. Regardless, by this stage many are feeling financially secure. We each know several women in their late forties

> "Whenever I need motivation, all I have to do is look around at my fellow employees. I feel their enthusiasm and it is infectious. Their ability to motivate me ensures I keep motivating them."
>
> Cindi Bigelow '86

to mid-fifties who were on the threshold of the C-suite, stopped and said, "That's it. I'm out. I've hit my number. I'm going to start spending my time in ways that are more meaningful to me personally."

A 2017 study by Egon Zehnder, a global executive search and consulting firm, sheds some light. They examined the careers of 7,000 women across seven countries, including the United States. They found that the higher a woman advanced in a company, the less likely she was to want an executive position. Only 57 percent of the women who had reached senior middle management roles still expressed a desire to go forward and claim a C-suite position, compared to 74 percent at the start of their careers. Many respondents noted professional exhaustion and an unwillingness to fight the same battles of bias they fought earlier in their careers.[34]

This perspective may be shaped, in part, by the fact that women often take longer to get to this career pivot than do their male peers. A 2017 study of 57 women CEOs[35] by Korn Ferry reported that female CEOs were four years older (50.9) than male CEOs (46.8), and it took them 30 percent longer to reach the top job.[36] Interestingly, McKinsey research finds that women of color are more likely than Caucasian women to want the top jobs, yet report that they get less access to opportunities, face more barriers and experience even less upward mobility than their white female peers.[37]

Taking the C-Suite

Our experiences and interviews reveal three factors that affect whether a woman is open to taking the final leap into the C-suite. One is the **toll of the climb**. How weary is she coming out of the mid-career years? How taxing were the challenges encountered at work and at home? Does she have the energy for another round? A second is her **achievement motivation**. Is she still hungry and gunning to prove she can do more? Or is she feeling content with what she has achieved and beginning to look toward other horizons, perhaps in the non-profit or education sectors? Finally, there's the **opportunity cost**. Looking ahead, how "dear" a price would time in the C-suite exact on her partner's well-being, another family member's needs or perhaps her own desire for more dimensionality to her life?

For those deciding to press on, the benefits can be substantial, but the terrain continues to change. Similar to The Launch and The Mid-career Marathon phases, The Executive Transition requires a new level of people management skills, new types of business knowledge, as well as deeper strategic thinking and more nuanced relationship building.

People management

At the executive level, employees look to their leaders to articulate purpose, customers look to them to attest to product and service excellence, suppliers look to them for operating expertise and investors look to them to bring it all together to generate profits. People management at the highest levels is rooted in understanding the impact of your words and actions on those who report to you, work with you and learn from you.

Communications. At this level, it's all about spoken influence – one-on-one and in groups, both large and small. Talking to people is what C-suite jobholders do. For women on the threshold of the C-suite, finessing public speaking skills and finding a voice that is both strong and resonant with your personality should be a top development priority. The goal is to articulate a narrative that provides clarity, focus and meaning to your employees' work and, when needed, inspires heroism.

The good news is that in the 21st century marketplace there is no "one size fits all" speaking style that leaders are expected to adopt. Whether in small or large groups, being authentic and articulate trumps any preconceived model of what a leader might look or sound like. The key is to uncover and refine *your* "voice" in front of employees, stakeholders, the media and investors. This means, for example, that introverts can do as well as extroverts because successful communications at the C-suite level is not about where you "get" your energy – it's about how you convey purpose and meaning and give energy and inspiration to others. That said, it's worth noting that successful leaders who are introverts carefully monitor the

toll that frequent interactions have on their energy reserves and develop calendar management strategies to allow time for regrouping.

In public speaking, the most successful communicators combine natural aptitude with effort. They spend considerable time and effort strategizing with their teams on messaging, style and execution. If needed, they hire external coaches and seek out professional speechwriters to help them frame and craft their thoughts. Depending on the company and industry context, some may recruit partners to help them write and place pieces in select media outlets or engage strategically on social media.

Successful executive performance at this level also frequently includes stepping forward on national and international platforms on behalf of your company or industry; e.g., leading a project with a major trade association, taking a public platform with a speech at a conference or attending a convening like the World Economic Forum. These are high-profile venues where, once again, effective communication is key and, when done well, can catapult a person's reputation and agenda.

"For me, the shift between mid-career and executive happened organically when I went from being a mentor and manager — advising my team on how to complete tasks on my behalf — to being more of a leader and coach, somebody who gives them the tools and the confidence to identify the problems and seek the solutions themselves."

Sonali Lamba '12

Calendar management. Calendar setting may not seem like a significant senior executive task, but effective calendaring can make the difference between burnout, surviving or thriving in the C-suite. These are tough, fast-paced jobs. Time and energy are an executive's core assets. Managing your calendar effectively – in a manner that both prioritizes the right people and projects *and* leverages your energy ebbs and flows within a day and week – should be the top priority for you and your support team. Most senior executives function best when there is downtime for thinking each day and adequate transition time between meetings and speaking events. Psychological research shows that allowing appropriate transition time between tasks improves performance.[38] In applied terms, this is when a senior executive jots down notes, reflects on what just happened in meetings, returns phone calls or generates follow-up e-mails. Calendars need to be thoughtfully constructed to most effectively weather the long hours and performance demands of the C-suite.

Coaching and talent development.

Developing people and teams is core to performance in the C-suite. And it's *all* about coaching. There's not much "doing" at this level. As coaches, senior executives help their people articulate what success looks like, specify key performance indicators (KPIs) for monitoring and delivering performance and work proactively with them to catch mistakes early. In their own behavior, executives develop and finesse the art of asking questions, reflecting back what they hear and conveying confidence. They use directing and telling only when absolutely necessary.

Strong leaders understand the difference between coaching for individual performance and coaching for team performance. They learn to do both well. With their senior team, they set separate performance objectives for individuals versus the team as a whole. They allocate resources to support those objectives and smooth relations among members, if needed, to achieve team synergies. Most importantly, they know how to deliver tough feedback to people or teams in a timely and constructive manner, with both compassion and clarity.

Team management at the C-suite level also means overseeing the performance of cross-functional teams. These are groups of employees convened from across various leaders' units and charged with tackling some of the most vexing problems facing a company. Key to coaching these teams is helping them break complex problems into solvable components and specifying achievable timelines and deliverables. With cross-functional teams, keeping team members, who do something else as their primary job, focused on delivering solutions to a hard problem that can actually get implemented can help make (or break) a career.

"Earlier in your career, you deliver value by being a functional expert or an effective people manager. When you reach the C-suite, you have to focus on the entire business and how all the pieces come together to drive growth and shareholder value. So learn as much as you can about multiple functions on your way up, as you will need that knowledge and experience to be effective in executive leadership. "

Lisa Earnhardt '96

Business knowledge

C-suite executives understand what it takes to run a business. They have mastered the business function and market in which they started their careers. By now, they have acquired a solid grounding in several other core functions and markets. If for some reason there are important knowledge and experience gaps, now is the time to fill them in order to gain the perspective needed to see problems with an "enterprise-wide" view: one that is holistic, crossing functions, geographies and product lines. For example, if you have never launched a new product or worked in an international role, you may want to position yourself for assignments that will help you to gain those experiences.

With an enterprise-wide view in-hand, there are additional core skills that C-suite executives need. These center around managing a firm's market performance and reputation at the highest levels. Specific areas likely include:

Managing growth. Whether through organic means (by increasing revenue through more customers, more products, new markets or bigger tabs) or via acquiring new businesses and products, a core senior executive task is to partner with peers and teams to deliver continued growth – quarter by quarter, year by year.

The senior team is also accountable for delivering earnings to their shareholders. In addition to revenue, this means delivering margin improvements by using capital, labor and innovation investments and cost-cutting initiatives to achieve efficiencies and decrease costs over time.

Supporting investor relations. C-suite executives are often called on to support investor relations, in order to demonstrate that their company has strong senior management bench strength with the right plans and the right teams to deliver results. Back to the earlier points we made about the importance of communications skills: being able to convincingly and succinctly explain how your unit delivers value to shareholders is a core C-suite skill.

Staying close to the customer. Last but not least, the strongest C-suite executives never get too far from their front-line teams and customers. They make it a point to spend time in plants, distribution and call centers, with sales and marketing teams and in back offices – meeting employees, hearing their

stories and concerns. The same is true with customers. Many C-suite executives, even in support functions, regularly visit with customers to keep a pulse on their markets and their company's performance. Are customers happy? Do they truly understand the value you're trying to bring to them? Do employees four and five levels below you know why they do what they do every day?

Together these internal and external touches keep an executive connected with the core of the business.

"Learning to 'see around corners' is incredibly valuable. As I've progressed, I've found that people don't like to share troubling news. I've attempted to put myself where I'm more likely to be able to 'see'… skip-level meetings, conference participation, customer meetings, talent coffees or technology networking etc., so that I'm not blindsided."

Barbara B. Hulit '91

Dealing the with unexpected. Whether bad news emerges from internal sources (e.g., a plant or employee problem) or external sources (a customer incident, public branding misstep or a new proposed government regulation), senior executives need to own and address the non-routine issues that bubble up through the business units and functions they lead. Depending on the impact, seasoned executives know when to ask for help from legal, HR or corporate affairs, and, if needed, to bring in a broader team. If a situation could have company-wide ramifications, they need to determine if and when they elevate the issue to the CEO.

Strategic thinking

As one of the most senior leaders in an organization, it is not enough to manage operations and unexpected developments in order to deliver results each quarter. The best executives at this level also anticipate changes that may be needed to keep their company competitive for the future. This is when developing organizational and strategic knowledge over the full course of a career and keeping a pulse with customers and employees starts to pay off.

Core issues to be monitored and addressed center around organizational coherence and alignment. Is your company realistic about its competitors, the rate of change in your marketplace and the stage of development within your industry? Is the current organization designed in a way that maximizes customer connectivity, operational excellence and innovation, as well as employee engagement? The core tools for doing this include well-researched competitive analyses, as well as strategic and annual plans built in response to hard data on customers, competition and innovation. This is also the time to master the art of taking your team through regular operating reviews and assessing and improving employee engagement, making sure that your infrastructure is healthy and aligned with your strategy.

Competitive strategy insights may lead you to form a transaction team to buy or sell a business or create a joint venture; undertake a major organizational restructuring to create global category teams or merge two existing business units; or engage in a significant cost-cutting exercise. Whatever it is, the best senior executives demonstrate an ability to envision the strategic change their company needs, narrate their

thinking in a compelling way and build the processes necessary to bring others along. They then build and equip teams to deliver on the goal.

For some senior executives, if the CEO is supportive, the C-suite may be the time to join a corporate or high-profile non-profit board as a way of rounding out your business perspectives, strategic insights and understanding of governance. If that's not possible, the most forward-thinking executives take it on themselves to cultivate the habit of observing how a select group of companies approach strategy, innovation, growth and investor relations. It's easy to do by reviewing annual reports, 10Ks and analyst reports, and by listening to investor calls.

With the CEO. Whether you were hand-picked by your CEO or inherited, the key to a strong relationship is to understand what the CEO wants and needs from your role, his/her preferred communication and management styles and how he/she likes to hear about bad news. Savvy executives figure out as quickly as possible what the CEO expects from each leader on the senior team, how the CEO prioritizes the executive's own business unit and the vision for how that unit fits into broader operational and strategic goals. Your goal then is to align your and your unit's performance with your CEO's expectations, or if appropriate, to develop and persuade the CEO of an alternate plan.

Relationship building

By the time executives make it to the C-suite, most have built a strong network of relationships within and outside their company and industry. The final stage in successful relationship-building lies in refining peer and near-peer relationships at the highest levels of the organization and doing so in a way that creates smooth, low-drama interactions.

This phase has four foci, each of which involves building trusted relationships with different stakeholder groups. These include:

Within the top team. For members of the top management team, success is as dependent on fit as it is on performance. The talent, drive and ambition that propels executives into the C-suite often aren't what fuels success once there. Hard-charging, outspoken, performance-driven executives often find that they have to tamp down and change their style. Here smoothness, likeability and calm become important coping mechanisms for a team that has to deal with high-stakes problem-solving on a near daily basis. Fitting in to the flow, often in ways that are unspoken, becomes the relationship-building lesson.

For women, a core challenge comes in managing the tension between being seen as deal-maker versus straight shooter. Both are highly effective roles and beneficial to the

"The skills that get you through launch and mid-career are not the skills you need as an executive. Early in your career, there's a ton of very quantifiable ways to measure success. The challenge at the executive level is that the more senior you get, the softer, more amorphous and more nuanced the criteria become. I think that can be very hard for women. All the quantifiable things that you can point to in order to demonstrate value, all those things that have been enough until now, are no longer enough. At the executive level, likeability and support from peers play an increasingly dominant role in your upward mobility."

Anne Clarke Wolff '89

"In my career, I most often dealt with outside boards, which I sat on, and boards overseeing companies, which we invested in. What I learned from these experiences was that boards matter and that they operate differently from other senior teams. So, I'd encourage anyone considering a C-suite role to seek out board exposure – the earlier, the better."

Paula B. Pretlow '78

organization. Our experience and interviews found that the deal-maker is the predominate persona in the C-suite – a politically astute and pragmatic operator, willing to support a colleague on a project in exchange for their support on another. The straight shooter, in contrast, is a persona who speaks from what she sees as truth, rather than political expediency, especially when she perceives that the stakes for the organization are high. But doing so can incur a political cost, especially if no one else on the team is calling out the issue.

The straight shooter style is the way that many senior female executives we interviewed prefer to engage, but it can create negative perceptions, making it a harder road to walk. There aren't as many natural allies for this type of executive, beyond the CEO. Thus, figuring out how to balance the tension between collaborating and voicing dissent is key to smoothing relationships in the C-suite.

With the board. Some CEOs give their boards broad access to senior team members; others prefer to keep board interactions tightly controlled. Your goal as a C-suite member is to know your role and play within the parameters your CEO outlines. CFOs and general counsels, by the nature of their jobs, get more board access than do other team members. Regardless, when called on, you need to deliver for your CEO and the board. Since the board needs to approve material investments and strategic plans, they rely on senior executives to know the facts and have fully pressure-tested their proposals before they present. The boardroom is not the time or place to get creative or inspired.

Beyond your current role, since it is the board's job to select the next CEO, winning over the board is critical for those who aspire to land the top job. Interestingly, over the last 10 years, 72 percent of Fortune 500 female CEOs have been promoted from within.[39]

"When I'm searching for top talent, I work with the headhunters I know and trust. They've come to learn what I'm looking for and when they vouch for someone they know well, that candidate goes to the top of my list."

Suzanne Blaug '83

With headhunters. Whether or not an executive plans to switch companies at the senior executive level, cultivating relationships with the best headhunters in your industry and function is a wise strategy. Yet many women fail to invest in these relationships, creating a competitive disadvantage. Having good outside options boosts your confidence at work and your strength as a negotiator. Plus markets change, politics change and with that, plans can change – yours or your company's. For example, if a sudden CEO transition puts someone in the top job who is not your ally it's good to have back-up options, or when an outside opportunity that is really is too good to pass up comes along, you want to be the candidate. For these reasons and more, it's prudent to be known and respected by key headhunters.

Conclusion

If we are going to get more women into the C-suite and other significant leadership positions, we need more women to stay in the full-time workforce through each of the three pivot points: launching well post college, thriving during mid-career years and making the transition into the C-suite. Even among the women who make it through The Launch and The Mid-career Marathon, not all decide to make the final pivot into the C-suite. But for those who do, the benefits are significant. They range from financial gains, to opportunities for impact and personal growth, to the importance these women hold as role models for the men and women coming up behind them.

Whether one is a woman or man, C-suite roles are more nuanced and higher risk than earlier roles because of their scale and visibility. The stakes at this level are high, and performance is public. Women are still rarer and, as a result, more visible when they take senior roles. And our society is still generating a collective understanding of how strong female leaders look, speak and behave.

Women who succeed in the C-suite are still fighting the spoken and unspoken battles that being a minority requires. But if you believe, as we do, that getting more women into business and succeeding at the highest levels are important for our organizations, our economy, our country and our world, then we need more women to persevere. We need to assure that women are reaching the C-suite in ever-closer proportions to men and that they are thriving along the 25- to 40-year journey that a successful C-suite career requires.

To do this, we need all stakeholders to place more attention on identifying the impediments facing women at each phase and to apply greater intention in overcoming them. This means the women themselves, the men they work with and for, our corporate leaders and our boards. We all must keep our eyes open and hearts and minds all-in.

How they successfully navigated The Executive Transition

THEY BUILT STRONG TEAMS.

"At the executive level, it's more about how good my team is, not just how good I am. That had never really occurred to me before. But as a senior leader, it really is about ensuring that I've got the best team and that they really know what they're doing. That way, I feel comfortable stepping away and letting them have the limelight. I don't even review every detail of what they're presenting to the CEO anymore. They're that good." SUZANNE BLAUG '83

THEY FOUND INSPIRATION TO KEEP GOING.

"Early in my career, when I was first learning about the Kevlar business while walking a manufacturing line down in Spruance, Va., I stopped one of the workers and said, 'What do you do here? Tell me about your job.' And he said, 'Ma'am, I save lives.' At first I thought, well, that's a little cheeky. But then I started thinking. Here was an individual who was so proud of what he did as an operator on the line. He felt that he saved lives - and he did, because of the quality of the material and what it meant to the military and to the first responders, to have those vests. That kind of pride made me want to make that business even more successful. I got my energy by seeing what our people were doing and how they were approaching tough problems. As I moved up, whenever I would get down or feel frustrated, I would go on the road to remind myself what the power of DuPont really was." ELLEN KULLMAN '83

THEY CONNECTED WITH CUSTOMERS.

"My dad died about 10 years ago and even though he wasn't really involved in the business any longer, there were a lot of questions about what was going to happen to the company. I couldn't believe it! I thought, what do people think has been going on here? So, I went on the road. I visited all my customers. I told them things were fine. I explained that I'd been running the company for a while, that we had a capable advisory board and that they were paying attention. What I found was that I just had to look people in the eyes and say, 'It's okay. I'm here and have been working with you.' It was all fine in the end, but I was shocked by the lack of understanding and trust, and I realized I needed to get out there more." ANN DRAKE '84

THEY MADE BOLD MOVES INTO NEW MARKETS.

"Getting into the U.S. market on the brand side of the business was a transformational move for our company. I had been an integral part of building the plan myself. But despite careful thinking, we quickly found that a number of our assumptions were challenged. We were now in a fight for market share with heavyweights like Abbott and Bristol-Myers Squibb. What we learned very quickly was that we needed a niche strategy to differentiate ourselves and to ensure our share of voice would count. To make this work, there were some days when I wore the hat of a salesforce leader and others when I wore the hat of the marketing leader. I listened and learned firsthand from physicians about what would make a difference. And I made changes that paid off. By the end of year two, we broke even with the product; in year three, we turned a profit. With bold moves like these and strong execution, we took the organization from zero to more than a billion dollars this past year." VINITA GUPTA '92

THEY DEALT WITH BIAS.

"As a leader in a philanthropic organization, I have had the opportunity to work with many young women and men who face daily obstacles based on their gender or race or sexuality – young people who experience discrimination at the individual and system level. They are often told explicitly or implicitly what they can and can't do. In a sense, they are told that their story has been written. As a gay person, I am a member of a discriminated class. As a woman, I am a member of a discriminated class. And so I have experienced others trying to write my story. But I said, 'No, it is my story. I will determine what I have to bring to the table and find a way to push through the noise.' This is a message that I share widely with young people. Don't ever let someone else write your story or define your path because of one piece of who you are. If you are a young girl who dreams of a job in an industry with few woman role models, go for it!"
WENDY NELSON '99

THEY INVESTED IN THEIR PEOPLE.

"You make some of your own luck. But you're not an island. The people of your organization are the heart and soul and what make everything happen. So you need to make the time and effort to really invest properly in your people. Make sure that you not only have the right team, but that they feel supported. They have the training, the assets, whatever it is they need." KEECH COMBE SHETTY '06

THEY BUILT SUPPORTIVE MARRIAGES.

"My husband and I have been able to make dual careers work. At one point he was a CEO; at one point we were both CEOs. It has been an enormous challenge. Who you choose as a partner makes a huge impact on whether you can make dual careers work. I was incredibly lucky to have a husband who went into it saying, 'We're going to make this work for two people.' We both made trade-offs. We made family a priority. We took all our vacations. We communicated, communicated, communicated. And we were both comfortable doing any role." BETSY D. HOLDEN '82

THEY INVESTED IN RELATIONSHIPS.

"There's no way I would have started this business if I hadn't found an amazing business partner. There are several screens you can run early in that relationship to figure out if this is going to work or not. Since you really don't want to waste time, I think having the difficult conversations up front is super important. But even doing that, the truth is you still have to work on this relationship, as much I think as I work on my marriage at times. It's important to acknowledge and respect that the relationship you have with your business partner is as important as the business, particularly when you have a lot of employees watching that dynamic constantly." NICOLE STAPLE '12

THEY KNEW WHEN IT WAS TIME TO REST.

"When I hit 55, I was burned out. It started at about 25 percent of the time, it grew to 50 percent, it grew to 70 percent. I was just burned out. I needed a rest, my body was tired, so I gave my firm about eight months notice that I was going to retire because I wanted to be involved in helping find my replacement. Then, a month before I was due to retire, I learned that I was very seriously ill. I had a very rare form of breast cancer. Had I not listened to my body, had I not listened to that burned-out feeling, I would be dead. Period. End of story."
PAULA B. PRETLOW '78

What are the best parts of being in a senior leadership position?

I love the impact, the ability to create strategy and deliver. Having a great deal of influence over the organization's direction. **Showing that women can do the job.** Having control and being able to shape the culture of an organization. **Being a role model for young women.** Inspiring, leading and driving strategic change. **I'm good at it!**

What are the worst parts of being in a senior leadership position?

Time away from home, never being able to unplug. Constantly having to deal with gender stereotypes and walk the line between being likeable and being competent. **Being expected to do more than a male counterpart.** Expectations of me that may not fit my goals. **Feeling underqualified for the position.** As you move up there is a risk/tendency to lose touch with the core skills that drove you to love your job and be successful in the first place. **The importance of soft skills, even over expertise or technical mastery.** How challenging the politics of the organization are. There's an unwritten set of rules no one tells you about in advance. **It's more about how you work with others than actual performance.** The degree of sexism. Most CEOs are men and surround themselves with other men. Strong women are seen as aggressive and too emotional. **Men who are less qualified, with lesser work ethics, are promoted and provided development opportunities.** That it's me in this role. I suffer from impostor syndrome. **How lonely it feels.**

If you could start your executive phase over, what would you do differently?

Focus on establishing strong peer networks and more team cohesions, because cohesion drives results over the long run. Network more and have more self-confidence – I am a rock star at work and for some reason, I never feel that I'm good enough – I see men who are half as capable think they are rock stars even when they're not. **Get a business coach earlier – it has been very effective in moving me up to the C-level in the past few years.**

What do you believe is the greatest barrier preventing women from getting to the C-suite?

That it requires a life of zero balance to get there. **Not being able to balance it all or not seeing the personal sacrifices (extra hours, extra stress, extra politics, etc.) as worth the work rewards.** Family obligations. Women carry the bulk, if not all the mental load, are expected to be the catchall/default for all things at home, etc. Ten years post-MBA with two kids, I find myself unable to put as much effort into work and am constantly feeling drained, despite having help. That lack of energy makes the path to the C-suite longer, if not unattainable. **Women question whether they can do a job; men just jump in.** Discrimination against women who work part-time while they bring up children. This delays your career advancement and then it's difficult at an older age to get back on track. Most organizations are not flexible enough for this. **Women don't want to be in the C-suite as it currently operates. All the teamwork and collaboration that gets you to the top is not how the top operates.** Desire to have a bigger impact on the lives of their children. It is the only reason I left my career path. While my husband is a capable father, he does not have the same intuition or concerns about our children. I think for many women, priorities shift when they have kids. Many very smart, very ambitious, very successful women find their emotions become much more complex after becoming mothers. **The social barrier – the ease of getting lunch, drinks or beer or playing soccer or fantasy football.** These relationships build informally and break the tie between two equally good performers of different genders. It's a boy's club. There are unwritten rules that prevent women from succeeding. I don't think men are purposefully discriminating, but lots of work gets done in the boy's room, on the golf course, at basketball games and bars. Typically, we don't get invited to these events. Additionally, there aren't enough women who are mentors to help others succeed. **Culture and having the right mentors.** Not navigating politics effectively. Men on the team are able to have failures and recover; women don't have that luxury. One misstep and there are consequences. **Leadership attributes and actual performance still being viewed differently.** Bias in team-building events. At my old company, I was the only senior woman and they insisted on doing team-building golf, which I did not play. Lack of access to conversations, interactions and networks outside their immediate roles. **Promotion criteria are applied differently between genders and applied increasingly in more subjective ways.**

Last word on The Executive Transition

"Just be yourself. So often when we take on these really big jobs, we think that we have to change. Not that we don't have to use more influence rather than direct control – there's a lot of things like that, which do change – but **if you try to be somebody you're not, you will not be as successful as if you are who you are**." ELLEN KULLMAN '83

"Someone who I really respected once told me, **'Pros don't panic.'** It is critical as a leader that you remain calm. That does not mean you cannot be very energetic, but especially during difficult times, I try to never forget that people are watching. You have to always remember that fact." CINDI BIGELOW '86

"**Whatever your mind can conceive and believe, it can achieve.** When you see that glass ceiling that everyone talks about, remember it's just glass. You can see through it, you can break through it, it's no big deal. You can make it happen." VINITA GUPTA '92

"If you don't negotiate, if you don't advocate for yourself, if you don't take the risks and the opportunities, then the women who are behind you have no role models. They don't have the opportunity to see that this is something they can do, too. **If you don't negotiate for your salary, then the woman coming in behind you just had to set her anchor lower.**" KATHLEEN L. MCGINN '92

"**Leave everything better than when you found it.** Sometimes this can be a really important, momentous thing and sometimes it can be something super small. But you have to figure out a way to make it better." KATHY ELSESSER '93

"At the end of the day, the buck stops with you. Learning that has really forced me to focus on what matters, whether it be driving value for our customers, driving value for our shareholders or driving value for our employees. That's **the benefit of drinking from the firehose each and every day: you learn to pick a few things and do them really well.**" LISA EARNHARDT '96

"**Listen with intentionality** for clarity and understanding. Don't take yourself so seriously that you dismiss or diminish the suggestions and opinions of others who may differ from you." ROSLYN M. BROCK '99

"There was a time when people would advise you to leave your personal life at home and bring your work self to the office. The danger in following that advice too closely is that you don't lead with vulnerability or build trust. **For your team to take risks with you they have to trust you, and to trust you they have to know you.** So think about what you are willing to reveal." WENDY NELSON '99

"**It's important for women to understand where their strength is and to compete on their strength.** When we dwell on our weakness, we allow what we perceive as our weaknesses to slow us down." JENNY LEE '01

"Have a sense of self professionally before entering a big role, whether it's in a family business or an executive role in a large company. Women shy away from roles and say, 'I'm not completely prepared for that, so I'm not ready.' Meanwhile men jump in. **It's important to feel that sense of comfort professionally and to not sell yourself short.**" KEECH COMBE SHETTY '06

"Many entrepreneurs are more risk-averse than some might think. Launching a business is of course risky. But a lot of things are risky. I'm terrified of flying and I fly every week. I've learned that it's more about **getting comfortable in uncertain environments.**" NICOLE STAPLE '12

CHAPTER 5

SUMMIT INSIGHTS

The first Kellogg Global Women's Summit, May 8-9, saw us hosting nearly a thousand women "live" at the Global Hub in Evanston, as well as hundreds more at extension events around the world, and a thousand more via livestreaming. There were 30 panels featuring nearly 80 world-class speakers, who shared their insights and inspired participants with their stories.

The focus of the Summit was on educating, equipping and inspiring more women to stay in the pipeline all the way to the C-suite because we'll all benefit when more women achieve their highest potential and experience the meaning and impact that can come from a sustained career trajectory. In the process, the Summit helped forge new connections, form new friendships and foster a deeper sense of urgency and collective accountability.

In this chapter, we present highlights from many of the panels so that even more people can benefit from the wisdom of these wonderful women.

A Conversation with Hollywood Leading Lady, Sherry Lansing

Sherry Lansing was the first woman to head a major film studio when she was appointed president of 20th Century Fox in 1980. During her nearly 30 years in Hollywood, she was the driving force behind so many iconic films, including Academy Award winners *Forrest Gump*, *Braveheart* and *Titanic*, not to mention *Fatal Attraction*, *The Accused* and *Indecent Proposal*. Throughout her film career, Lansing earned a reputation as a trailblazer. Her 12 years as Chairman and CEO of Paramount Pictures resulted in an unprecedented period of creative and financial success for the studio. From film to philanthropy, Sherry Lansing has truly earned the title Leading Lady.

"All I wanted was to be an actress. I was so naive at the time, but sometimes that really holds you in good stead because it doesn't allow you to see the obstacles."

"My dad had a very small real estate business. Soon after he died, two men came to my mother and said, 'Margot, you don't need to worry, we'll take care of you.' I can still see my mother in the middle of crying, she looked at them with these steely eyes and she said, 'No you won't. You will teach me how to run the business and I will take care of my family.' In that moment, at 8 years old, I saw everything I needed to know. I saw that you could learn to do something, you could be taught. And I also saw that you must never be a victim."

"I think the way to survive pressure is to stay focused on the job, because if you let all the noise out there affect you, you can't function."

"You have to decide what creates a happy life. Life is about choices. It's about chapters and choices. You can have it all sequentially, but it's very hard to have it all at the same time. Make your own choice about when things happen."

Sherry Lansing NU '66, Founder and CEO, The Sherry Lansing Foundation; Former Chairman and CEO, Paramount Pictures; Subject of the book, *Leading Lady: Sherry Lansing and the Making of a Hollywood Groundbreaker*

A CONVERSATION WITH HOLLYWOOD LEADING LADY, SHERRY LANSING

SHERRY LANSING NU '66
Founder and CEO, The Sherry Lansing Foundation
Former Chairman and CEO, Paramount Pictures
Subject of the book, *Leading Lady: Sherry Lansing and the Making of a Hollywood Groundbreaker*

SALLY E. BLOUNT '92
Dean, Kellogg School of Management, Northwestern University
Board member, Abbott Laboratories, Ulta Beauty, Inc. and The Joyce Foundation

How Bold Moves Can Make Your Career

We've all heard about the importance of taking risks if you want to get ahead. This is especially true if you want to rise quickly and make it all the way to the top. Doing what others can't or won't is guaranteed to get you noticed. Nearly every C-suite woman we know can tell you about a time she made a bold move and how it paid off – short term and/or long term – whether it was launching a new product or service, executing a turnaround or taking on an overseas assignment.

Summary A bold move requires two elements: an "out of the ordinary" job change with the potential to make a substantial positive difference to your organization and, by extension, to your career. Making a bold move typically delivers at least four key benefits. It increases your visibility, speeds your learning, proves your willingness to step up when needed and demonstrates you have key qualities a C-suite leader needs, including smart risk-taking, confidence and grit.

"Whenever I'm facing the decision about whether to make a bold move, I think about standing at the edge of a precipice and I ask myself: What is the worst thing that could happen and could I live with it? Then I think, what's the best thing that could happen and does that really excite me? In the end, if you can live with the worst case and the best case is appealing, then just jump. The rest will take care of itself."

Perry Yeatman, Founder and CEO of Your Career, Your Terms; CEO of Perry Yeatman Global Partners LLC; Former executive, Unilever, Kraft Foods and Burson-Marsteller

"There's a wonderful acronym for fear: 'False expectations appearing real.' It's easy to imagine the worst happening. So, when faced with a bold opportunity, it's very important that you ask yourself three questions: What is it that I want to happen? What are the likely things that could preclude that? And who's on the team that's going to help me get there?"

Connie L. Lindsey, Executive Vice President and Head of Corporate Social Responsibility and Global Diversity & Inclusion at Northern Trust, Chicago; Former National Board President, Girl Scouts of the USA

"My mother told me, 'You don't have to compromise to be recognized. Your gifts will make room for you.' So, know who you are, know what the risks and opportunities are and know that when you make this move, it's going to give you some sort of fulfillment. Then, trust your gut and be willing to stand up and have faith that you can make a difference."

Roslyn M. Brock '99, Vice President, Advocacy & Government Relations, Bon Secours Health System Inc.; Chairman Emeritus, NAACP

"I always ask myself: 'If I am acting with intent, what choice would I make now versus just letting my life move forward without any intervention?' And, if it's important, I just do it."

Betsy Ziegler, CEO, 1871; Former Chief Innovation Officer, Kellogg School of Management

Letting Go of Perfection

Many women strive for perfection – trying to act and even look perfect, both at work and at home. We do this because we believe it's a positive characteristic, perhaps even the "right" thing to do. In fact, quite the opposite is true. Research shows striving for perfection can actually hold us back, making us more reluctant to take important risks, raise our hands when we have questions or contributions to share or go for a promotion when we feel anything less than 100 percent certain we can succeed. Seeking perfection limits our self-advocacy and authenticity as we prioritize others' perceptions over our own. But how do you let go of the perfection mindset and succeed as your authentic self?

Summary The road to recovery from perfectionism is really more of an art than a science. It takes recognition of the expectations that we have for ourselves, many times due to our past, in order to make the choice to give ourselves a break. You have to: find the willpower to dive in; create tools that get you through the inevitable rough spots; understand that your definition of perfection will change over time; and learn what makes you happy.

"The idea of 'Letting go of perfection' assumes that you had perfection to let go of at one point. What is perfect? Perfect can mean a lot of different things at different times to different people. So, what I feel blessed to do right now is to help young women understand all the different ways they can be 'perfect' by their own definition."

Elizabeth P. Schuster '10, President, Regina Dominican High School; Founder, Samadhi; Former executive, Vanguard

LETTING GO OF PERFECTION

GLORIA GUEVARA '09
President & CEO, World Travel and Tourism Council (WTTC)
Former Secretary of Tourism for Mexico

SARAH PERSONETTE NU '01
COO, Refinery29
Board member, Build-a-Bear Workshop
Former Vice President, Global Business Marketing at Facebook

ELIZABETH P. SCHUSTER '10
President, Regina High School
Founder, Samadhi
Former executive at Vanguard

MARY B. CRANSTON (MODERATOR)
Retired Senior Partner and Chair Emeritus, Pillsbury Winthrop Shaw Pittman LLP
Board member, Aretec, Boardspan, Chemours, CSAA Insurance Group, MyoKardia and Visa

"I deploy this concept of 'start by starting.' If somebody on my team brings me an idea, I say, 'Let's just start! Let's see what this looks like.' I can give you countless examples from launching new digital channels in my 20s to being on a publicly traded board in my 30s, where this has worked. A lot of it is about giving people the confidence to take the first step. It's connected to the concept of failing fast and celebrating failures and not being afraid of falling down."

Sarah Personette NU '01, COO, Refinery29; Board member, Build-a-Bear Workshop; Former Vice President, Global Business Marketing, Facebook

"Even though I had been promoted to the highest levels, my mind began to torture me about how I wasn't good enough. I couldn't stop those thoughts, but I did come to understand that I didn't have to believe them. I found two strategies to cope: one, I kept taking baby steps, and two, I began a daily meditation that opened up a field of wisdom behind all the mental processing."

Mary B. Cranston, Retired Senior Partner and Chair Emeritus, Pillsbury Winthrop Shaw Pittman LLP; Board member: Aretec, Boardspan, Chemours, CSAA Insurance Group, MyoKardia and Visa

"At the end of the day, perfection is being happy. For me, that's enjoying my kids, enjoying my work. Your idea of perfection needs to be flexible."

Gloria Guevara '09, President & CEO, World Travel & Tourism Council (WTTC); Former Secretary of Tourism for Mexico

Survive, Thrive and Sexual Drive Across Your Life

Women often take care of everyone else but ignore their own health and critical warning signs. What can you do to prevent, diagnose and treat critical women's health issues? And, why are so many of these issues, and even issues relating to our sex lives, often overlooked by health professionals?

Summary The disparity between how society funds male and female health, including sexual health, is striking. Women are underrepresented in clinical trials and their symptoms are not taken as seriously. Even so, women must push their health issues and concerns, whether it is about sex, cardiovascular disease or osteoporosis, ask questions and engage in meaningful conversations with trusted practitioners.

"In 1991, the New England Journal discovered that there is a disparity about how men and women are treated for cardiovascular disease. Before then, there had been a general assumption that women didn't get cardiovascular disease. Data showed that when men and women came in with chest pain, the women were sent home with Tums and the men were sent to the CAT lab and had angioplasty or surgery. But women are at risk. One out of every three women is going to be affected by cardiovascular disease. Twice as many women are going to die of heart disease and stroke than all cancer deaths combined. So, we still need to be talking about this. There are still disparities."

Marla A. Mendelson FSM '88, Cardiologist and Associate Professor of Medicine and Pediatrics, Northwestern Feinberg School of Medicine and Northwestern Memorial Hospital; Founder and Director of the Center for Women's Cardiovascular Health of the Bluhm Cardiovascular Institute, the Northwestern Heart Disease and Pregnancy Program, the Northwestern Adult Congenital Heart Program and the Marfan Center

"Look at the woman next to you. One of you is going to have a fracture due to osteoporosis after the age of 50. And once you've had one fracture, your risk is five times greater to have another fracture within a year. From the day I turned 40, my doctor was all over me about having a mammogram, having a colonoscopy. But nobody ever told me to have a bone density scan. They recommend screening for low-risk women at the age of 65. I perceive myself to be a low risk woman, we have no family history, I exercise religiously. But when I had my scan done, I had osteoporosis. If you aren't aware that you're at risk, it can go undetected."

Suzanne Blaug '83, Senior Vice President for Global Marketing and Commercial Development, Amgen

"Is there a double standard for sexual dysfunction? Absolutely. What can you do about it? Get more sleep. For every hour increase in sleep, there's an increase in the odds of having sexual intercourse. If the only thing that vibrates is your cellphone, it's time to go shopping. Over 50 percent of women use vibrators to reach orgasm and many more use them with a partner."

Lauren Streicher, Associate Clinical Professor of Obstetrics and Gynecology, Feinberg School of Medicine, Northwestern University and Medical Director, Northwestern Medicine Center for Sexual Health and Menopause; Author, *Sex Rx: Hormones, Health and Your Best Sex Ever*

Being Your Own Boss; From the Gig Economy to Growing Your Own Big Business

According to the National Association of Women Business Owners, there are now more than 9.4 million firms owned by women in the U.S., generating $1.5 trillion in sales, and nearly three million of those are majority-owned by women of color. Indeed, women-owned firms account for 31 percent of all privately held firms. That's great news, especially in light of the less positive news coming out from other workplaces – from the gender pay gap to sexual harassment. Whether you're looking for the freedom of the "gig" economy or looking to build, scale and lead your own big business, there are literally millions of women out there who can help show you the way.

Summary Being your own boss has clear advantages, but it has downsides too. So, it's important to be clear from the start: 1) Why are you doing this/what is your primary motivation? 2) Why do you think it's right for you – are you a risk taker? Are you self-motivated? 3) Do you have a thoughtful, reasonable operating plan covering how you'll secure funding, find customers, build your team, etc.?

"In 2012, I was a global corporate executive. I could make seven figures a year and wear St. John's suits. Then, my 5-year-old said to me, 'Mommy, I really think it's time for you to be the boss of me.' That stopped me in my tracks. I'd had an amazing 25-year career up to that point and I expected to have at least two decades more. But I only had a few years before my daughter would be largely independent. I didn't want to miss that window. So, I decided to step down and go out on my own. Why did I think I could do it? First, I had 15 years of consulting experience prior to going corporate. So, I knew how to be a consultant and I knew I could attract clients – you only need a few anchor clients to make a decent living as a sole practitioner. But I also cut our routine expenses about 50 percent and decided to go it alone – doing everything myself from the strategic planning to the invoicing. This kept my costs low and my availability for Kirsten high. It does get lonely sometimes and I'm really tired of the paperwork, but I can pay all our bills, do great work and be the mom I want to be. So, on balance, it's totally been worth it."

Perry Yeatman, Founder and CEO of Your Career, Your Terms; CEO of Perry Yeatman Global Partners LLC; Former executive, Unilever, Kraft Foods and Burson-Marsteller

"I call myself an accidental entrepreneur. I spent three years working abroad, then came back to Chicago at a time when my friends were having children. They were dealing with a lot of mom guilt around the inability to prep good lunches for their children. So, I started packing lunches for my friends. That got me thinking…this has to be a problem for others too. Based on that insight, I did a Facebook ad to a local moms group. In two hours, 400 people had signed up for a service that didn't even exist. But I didn't just leap blindly. I said, what are the things I need to do to feel comfortable running this business? One was I needed to be able to pay myself. So, I had to convince people I was a worthwhile investment. To do that, I needed data. I spent six months actually prepping and delivering food and collecting data about who was coming back to us, how much they were paying, etc. And I decided I wanted to build a big business so I was willing to pursue VC funding. Once I had made those decisions was I ready to fully commit."

Rebecca Ann Sholiton '16, Co-Founder and CEO, Wise Apple

"I always tell other entrepreneurs, all you've got is an idea. Anyone who's going to join an idea has to have a lot of faith in you and your idea. So, when hiring employees, be flexible. Don't get caught up on whether they have experience in your specific industry. Look for someone who can solve problems."

Kara Goldin, Founder and CEO, Hint Inc.

"I didn't start out planning to build one of the largest female-owned consulting companies in the world. But, during the past three decades, APCO Worldwide has grown into a global consulting firm, operating in about 30 countries and employing about 800 people. And we did it organically, largely building every office from scratch. I don't know if passion was a greater incentive or fear. But I do know that when your clients and employees are counting on you, that's very motivating. And when you solve problems for people and create opportunities, there's no greater feeling."

Margery Kraus, Founder and Executive Chairman, APCO Worldwide

Generating Capital for Female Founders and CEOs

Money is the life blood of business. Without capital, businesses can't grow and thrive. When it comes to raising funds, female entrepreneurs have clearly been at a disadvantage. We've all seen the stats: Women get less than 3 percent of venture capital dollars even though the results demonstrate that they produce a 20 percent higher return than male entrepreneurs. Female founders and CEOs face unique challenges in raising capital but some savvy investors are trying to change the odds.

Summary There was a study published in the Harvard Business Review, looking at the questions investors ask female entrepreneurs versus the questions they ask male entrepreneurs. Two-thirds of the time, the questions the women were asked fell into the category of 'prevention' questions about managing risk, such as how they were planning to get to break even? Two-thirds of the time, the questions the men were asked were about promotion and growth. 'What's your path to $100 million in revenue?' The companies that were asked the prevention questions raised a mere one-fifth of the money compared to the companies that were asked the promotion questions. So the question for us is: How can we change that dynamic? And the answer is: Understand the process, ask for help, identify sponsors and know the answers to the tough questions before you get in the room.

"Investors make a decision whether or not they want another meeting within 20 minutes of the first meeting. But that's all you need. You're not trying to get a check during the first meeting. You're just trying to get to the next meeting."

Sutian Dong, Partner, Female Founders Fund

"I'm not good at asking for help. But you have to ask for help. You cannot do it alone. And when looking for people to help you, say yes to every breakfast and every coffee, no matter how many pounds you gain."

Trish Lukasik, CEO and Board Member, Luxury Garage Sale; Board member: Sargento Foods Company, NatureBox, Aspire and WTTW

"There are people who will help you. There are people, male and female, who have been around the community a long time and are just waiting for you to ask for their help and expertise."

Karin D. O'Connor '89, Clinical Assistant Professor of Innovation & Entrepreneurship, Kellogg School of Management

"Investors want to know you're going to be the one to push through a wall. One of the things I do really well is not give up. I'll break through walls to make things happen, and you can tell in a meeting with me, if I take your money, I will act like it's my money."

Rebecca Ann Sholiton '16, Co-Founder and CEO, Wise Apple

"I think it's really important for entrepreneurs to understand the investment thesis, the motives, the priorities and the return hurdles for their investment base."

Andrea Turner Moffitt, Co-Founder, Plum Alley Investments; Author, *Harnessing the Power of the Purse: Winning Women Investors*

"Answer questions about risk in a way that addresses the risk, but then pivot and make sure you do more promotional discussions as well."

Lisa Earnhardt '96, President and CEO, Intersect ENT; Board member: Intersect ENT and Nevro

Negotiating for Yourself on Your Way In, Up and Out

Much research has demonstrated that women do not negotiate for themselves. This is not because women cannot negotiate. Women often outperform men when it comes to negotiating on behalf of their companies and when they are negotiating for others, but they fail to negotiate for themselves.

Summary We only get what we ask for, yet women often don't negotiate for what they really want. There are three critical points of negotiation for women: on your way into the organization, on your way up through the organization and on your way out of the organization— whether that's by your choice or someone else's. Each of these situations are negotiable, and it's important that women feel empowered to ask for what they deserve and that they know how to best represent themselves and their accomplishments.

"Women actually often negotiate better than men when it comes to negotiating on behalf of an organization, on behalf of a charity or on behalf of their kids. They negotiate fiercely on behalf of others, but they don't negotiate on behalf of themselves. We need to negotiate for ourselves the way we would for others."

"You want to lead the discussion whenever you can but you can never negotiate until you have an offer."

"In all employment negotiations, you have some common objectives: address the other side's pressing business needs, make sure you differentiate yourself, establish and build a relationship with the other side and show how you aren't establishing precedent for the employer. Their biggest concern is not what they do for you, it's about what they would have to do for everybody else. You should have at least one negotiable issue on the table for every one of these objectives. You should never have a "salary negotiation," instead it should be a broad discussion focused on your role in meeting the company's needs, the timeline, the responsibilities, how success will be measured, and your package."

"Find what differentiates you. When you're different, you're worth more."

"Be bold in what you ask for!"

Victoria H. Medvec, Adeline Barry Davee Professor of Management and Organizations and Co-Founder and Executive Director, Kellogg Center for Executive Women, Kellogg School of Management

Succeeding and Leading in a Biased World

Bias is everywhere – bias about age, gender, race, religion, nationality, orientation and socio-economic status. Whether we recognize it or not, we are all biased by our upbringings, work experiences and perceptions. Learning to recognize and manage bias is key to successful team work. This important discussion shared real world experiences regarding what works to empower us individually and as leaders in our workplaces when facing bias. It also covered how to identify and understand your own blind spots so you can influence your thoughts, and in turn, your colleagues' perceptions in order to become a more inclusive leader.

Summary Everyone is biased and if we claim that we are not, we're lying to ourselves and others. There will be times in your career when bias will impact you and times when you will have to recognize your own bias against others.

"We learned the new 'F Word' is fear. We heard about the opportunity gap. We learned that you cannot change the place, if you're not at the place."

Megan Kashner '03, Clinical Assistant Professor of Public-Private Interface and Director of Social Impact, Kellogg School of Management

"Race still matters in this country. Gender still matters in this country. And orientation matters in this country. We all have bias, conscious and unconscious bias that we have to deal with. Because I am a woman of color does not mean that I can't discriminate. Anytime something happened to me in the workplace, I had to ask myself: 'Is it something I did? Is it something I said? Is it something about my performance?' and tick off those boxes and then ask, 'Is it something about me?' We have our own filters through which we see others. Oftentimes, we look in the mirror and ask others to act as we do. Instead we should use windows of opportunity to see difference."

Roslyn M. Brock '99, Vice President, Advocacy & Government Relations, Bon Secours Health System Inc.; Chairman Emeritus, NAACP

"When I was in my 20s, I was trying to become a district manager. One day I got a dozen roses from my boyfriend. My boss suggested that I should take them home because the decision-maker for the next district manager role would potentially see them, think that I wasn't fully committed and might not give me the job. That was a huge lesson. Perception really did matter and if we don't know the biases that are out there, we can't learn to impact or control them."

Ellen Taaffe '97, Clinical Assistant Professor of Leadership, Director of Women's Leadership Programs, Kellogg School of Management; Former executive, PepsiCo, Royal Caribbean and Whirlpool; Board member: John B. Sanfilippo & Son Inc. and Hooker Furniture Corporation

"Years ago, I was leading a team working for a large athletic company. We'd packed the team with competitive athletes but we also had two women who were not very athletic but had been doing really good work on the project. When the feedback came back, it was 'Love the team, love the advice, but we really want the whole team to be serious athletes.' I took a long time thinking about it but in the end I decided to take the women off the team. It was really hard. But I realized that I wasn't here to change that individual's moral compass. At the same time, I thought those women wouldn't succeed in that environment and it would have been even worse for them to fail. But I guaranteed them that the next great assignment that came in would absolutely be theirs. I'd kick anybody else off the team and make sure they got the opportunity. I also went to my team and I said, 'I want you to know that I'm not proud of where we came out.' It's about the opportunity gap. If you're going to change the fact pattern in the opportunity set, you have to figure out some other way to even the score."

Kathy Elsesser '93, Global Chair of the Consumer and Retail and Healthcare Groups, Goldman Sachs

What We Wish We Had Known: Lessons to and from Our Children

An impressive array of successful CEOs and senior leaders share what they learned across their careers and how their own experiences shaped the advice they gave their daughters. In return, some of their adult children reveal that working moms can often be amazing mothers, aunts and grandmothers too.

Summary Six very successful women shared advice they have offered to their children and lessons they have learned from their kids. In addition, three impressive Kellogg students revealed what they have learned from their moms. The inspirational panel was a great tribute to working moms, a reminder of the incredibly positive impact working moms have on their children and a wonderful way to celebrate Mother's Day!

"There's no doubt that part of the equation of defining what it all means is having children who see all the dimensions of who their parents are, and who understand that you might not be there every minute but you're there when it matters and you're there for real."

Edith W. Cooper '86, Former Partner and Global Head of Human Capital Management, Goldman Sachs; Board member: Etsy and Slack Technologies Inc.

"I tried to instill in my kids the understanding that they needed to do what they were afraid of. I tried to teach them not to let their fear stop them from doing what they wanted to do or being who they wanted to be."

Carol Lavin Bernick, CEO, Polished Nickel Capital Management; Board member: Northwestern Memorial HealthCare, BDT Capital Partners Fund Advisory Committee, Executive Committee of the Chicago Community Trust; Author, *Gather as You Go*

"Leadership is all about getting people to be the best that they can be."

Ilene S. Gordon, Executive Chairman, Ingredion Incorporated; Board member: Lockheed Martin and International Paper Company – Presiding Director

"Have the courage to create your own definition of success."

Betsy D. Holden '82, Senior Advisor, McKinsey & Company Inc.; Board member: Dentsply Sirona, Diageo PLC, Western Union and Lyons Magnus

"One of the best pieces of advice my mom gave me is to always go to the party. It's a reference to when she was in college and almost stayed home from a party where she actually met my dad. But it's a metaphor for how to approach life too. When you're on the fence about something—always go to the party. When you put yourself out there and take risks, that's when you grow."

Julie Holden '19, Full-time MBA Candidate, Kellogg School of Management

"If you're not happy with what's going on, the only person who can change it is you. Play the hand you want instead of the hand you were dealt."

Ellen Kullman '83, Co-Chair, Paradigm for Parity; Former Chair and CEO, DuPont; Board member: United Technologies Corporation, Dell Technologies, Amgen, Goldman Sachs and Carbon3D

"My mother always said you should take the job you can learn the most from."

Maggie Kullman '19, Full-time MBA Candidate, Kellogg School of Management

"My mother always challenged me to try something new."

Hannah Selonick '18, Full-time MBA Candidate, Kellogg School of Management

"Most profoundly, Hannah has said to me in heart-to-heart conversations, 'Don't have any regrets about being a perfectionist or anything else because everything you've done has brought you to where you are today.'"

Sona Wang '86, Founder and Managing Director, Ceres Venture Fund; Co-Founder, Chicago Blues Experience

Ten Things to Do Now to Set Yourself up for Long-Term Success (Sessions 1 & 2)

We all wish there was a silver bullet, that single thing we need to do to create the career and lives of our dreams. Sadly, there is not. But there are some key things – attitudes, attributes and actions – that research suggests can go a long way to making your career aspirations come true. In this session, leading consulting firms shared their top insights and tips based on years of research and real-world experience helping women succeed.

"There's no I in team. Build a great team around you and be comfortable with the idea of having people on your team who are different than you and challenge you. I've always tried to get the best people on my team because I know I have weaknesses and I need people to fill in those gaps."

Deborah DeHaas, Vice Chairman and National Managing Partner, Center for Board Effectiveness, Deloitte

"Pessimists look at situations and they say that they're personal, they're permanent and they're pervasive. Optimists say, no it's the situation. It's temporal, it'll pass. And they find ways to take something away from a bad situation and learn what they can do differently next time. Be an optimist."

Audrey C. Manacek NU '97, Senior Partner, McKinsey & Company

"Navigate with intent. You may want to do everything but if you know what gives you energy, what you want to focus on, it's easier to say things like, 'Actually that promotion isn't what I want.' Being really clear helps you make more intentional choices and can bring you more personal satisfaction."

Meghan J. Shehorn, Partner, Chicago, Bain & Company; Leadership Council Member, Civic Consulting Alliance; 2017 Working Mother of the Year, *Working Mother Magazine*

"Think about smart risks. Where is your opportunity to anticipate a need, find it and fill it? Sometimes that requires raising your hand before you think you're ready. Your male colleagues probably feel very comfortable doing that. Women need to feel comfortable too."

Melissa Cavanaugh, Head of Research and Content Strategy, Bersin by Deloitte

"Make your job work for you. And if the company you're at won't do that, find a different company. You are actually amazingly valuable. Take advantage of flexibility and use your voice."

Michelle Stohlmeyer Russell, Senior Partner and Managing Director, The Boston Consulting Group

"Really know who brings you energy versus who drains your energy. Then do everything you can to be with the people who actually bring you energy.

Be mindful of your health and wellbeing.

Stay in the workforce.

Go abroad or get experience working in a foreign market, even if working with a U.S. team.

Find a company that values you, and the things you care about."

Patricia A. Milligan '80, Senior Partner and Global Leader of When Women Thrive and Multinational Client Group, Mercer

Building Relationships with Intention and Value

Studies have shown that women trail men in developing connections that could help their careers. Women's networks tend to be smaller and less diverse than those of their male peers. As a result, women have less exposure to top-tier influencers and are less likely to hear about or put themselves forward for critical opportunities for advancement. As we move up, the breadth and depth of our networks becomes more important. Investing in relationships throughout your career and expanding your networks as you move up is an important support pillar for bigger career moves. This session featured women across industries sharing how they navigated through this tricky yet critical part of career development and advancement.

Summary Research suggests men spend more time networking and creating social capital. Research also says that men get more ROI on the time they spend networking. Women need to know how to navigate relationship building with intent and the same focus on ROI. Research also says that if you want to get promoted, the number one factor is your social capital, not your substantive skill set, proving who you know can many times be more important than what you know.

"I prefer to think of it as relationship building, rather than networking because you build relationships for all kinds of different purposes and outcomes. For me, it's often about energy and learning. If I leave a relationship or meeting and I feel like I learned things and got energy from it, then that would be high on my list of something to do again."

Ann Drake '84, Chairman and CEO DSC Logistics; Founder, AWESOME (Achieving Women's Excellence in Supply Chain Operations, Management and Education)

"At the risk of sounding too transactional, I tend to think of the 'capital' part of social capital almost like airline miles. You sort of deplete your units based on the asks that you make of people. Really high asks obviously deplete your bank more than smaller ones. But the way you build that bank back up isn't by meeting new people, it's by being reciprocal and giving back. My litmus test in the way I check myself is to look at that bank to make sure that I'm being as gracious as I can and giving back when people are asking me for help."

Sonali Lamba '12, Co-Founder, Brideside

"I have this belief that nobody can waste your time but you. You decide if you're going to meet somebody and if that interaction is useful. But there have to be times when you meet someone and say, without being rude, this is not it. You can't let the willingness to want to be liked get in the way of making progress. It took me a while to understand that you don't build relationships through hanging out. You build relationships because there's a shared experience, there's a give and a get. And that's got to be okay for you. If the relationship isn't there, it's got to be okay for you to say, I'm not going to let you waste my time."

Barbara B. Hulit '91, Senior Vice President, Fortive Corporation; Board member: Intersect ENT and Nevro

"When I was practicing law, I would go into a meeting and there would only be men there. They would talk about the Bulls or the Cubs or whatever. And my reaction was, 'What they are doing is excluding me.' I was the only woman and I already didn't have the social capital. What I realized eventually was that they were bonding, just by knowing the score of the game. It was so easy to just read the headlines of the sports page and be able to say one thing in the conversation and then you're in the club and you've bonded at that level. It took me a while to realize they weren't excluding me. It was a game that I was excluding myself from."

Jane DiRenzo Pigott, Managing Director, R3 Group LLC; Board member: VanEck Funds

Managing Well – Up, Down and Across

Managing well is critical to delivering your goals, advancing your career and building an engaging work environment. In this session, we explored the opportunities and pitfalls of relationships with peers, bosses and those that report to you. We also considered how role clarity, generational perspectives, communication styles and virtual work can all play a part in your ability to navigate and optimize your organizational effectiveness.

Summary As you move through The Mid-career Marathon, it becomes increasingly clear that the skills and talent that got you your initial raises and promotions won't necessarily carry you into the C-suite. Advancing in your career requires you to manage relationships with your subordinates, peers and superiors in creative ways that are increasingly productive for you and your team.

"We all like to work with people like us. But, I would challenge that. I've had a wonderful experience over the past few years working with our COO, someone totally different from me. I came from a very formal business school and consulting background whereas he had been with the company for 25 years and literally worked his way up from working at a restaurant. I can have all kinds of theoretical debates about what resources we need to get to our restaurants but that's totally different from getting into the environment with someone who has that direct experience."

Liz G. Williams '04, President, Taco Bell International; Board member: Orange County CASA (Court Appointed Special Advocate)

"Finding a goal you have in common with your team can be really useful. I was on a team where every time we would get into a meeting, the more senior boss would direct all questions to my direct boss, despite the fact he didn't know the answers. The more senior boss would also email instructions about the project to my direct boss, instead of giving them to me. I felt really undermined and frustrated. But instead of getting angry and calling him out, I tried to find something else that would get him to change his behavior. In the end, I positioned not coming to me directly as making us inefficient as a team. It worked and it was a great way to bring everybody back on the same page."

Tarra Sharp '13, Engagement Manager, McKinsey & Company

"I bring my whole self to work and I encourage everybody on my team to do the same. That doesn't mean I'm going to their children's birthday parties but it does mean that I'm aware of outside factors in their lives like an ailing parent or a new baby. The time you invest in that part of the relationship builds trust and that trust is fundamentally important to the working relationship because it allows us to have the tough conversations. You can't have those conversations if there's no foundational trust."

Carin L. Watson '04, Executive Vice Pesident, Learning and Innovation, Singularity University; Former Innovation Leader, Citi and Visa

"Ask for feedback when you want to give feedback, because someone giving you feedback gives you license to have that conversation."

Julie Hennessy '82, Clinical Professor of Marketing and Associate Chair of the Marketing Department, Kellogg School of Management

Top Three Reasons to Stay in the Game

At some point, almost everybody is tempted to step out – from a specific job or organization or from the workforce altogether. You hit a point where you feel the price is just too high or you simply can't succeed. Regrettably, this is a common experience. And, what you do about it has a striking impact on your future career prospects – a career that may stretch 40 years into the future for those launching now. So, before you throw in the towel, consider the top three reasons you should stay in the game and hear how others have managed to do just that.

Summary When *Working Mother* magazine conducted a survey called "Why do you work?" the number one reason women cited for working was money. But the number two reason was to use their skills and their education. They felt they had acquired these valuable assets and they didn't want to give them up, they wanted to develop them. Women need to stay in the game to 1) maintain their financial security, 2) feel the sense of accomplishment that comes with using their skills and 3) to avoid the negative career impacts that often haunt those who completely step out for prolonged periods of time.

"My mother stayed in an unhappy marriage because she was worried she couldn't pay the bills without my dad. I saw that and decided I didn't ever want to be with somebody for strictly financial reasons. I wanted to be with whomever I'm with because I care for them. To enable that, I made sure I could always support myself and my children."

Wendy Hufford, Chief Legal Operating Officer & VP, U.S. Litigation, Risk Management & Human Resources, Boehringer Ingelheim

"If I didn't work, my family couldn't pay our mortgage. I couldn't repay my student loans. I wouldn't be able to help out my parents. I think it is a luxury to debate, 'Should I stay in or not?' So, ask the question if you want, but don't feel like you need to. I love my job. Working has always been the assumption for me."

Meghan J. Shehorn, Partner, Chicago, Bain & Company; Leadership Council Member, Civic Consulting Alliance; 2017 Working Mother of the Year, *Working Mother Magazine*

"My three kids are grown. They're married. They're happy. I was a working mom. My daughter has two little girls. She works. I'm positive you can do it. If you're there for your kids when it counts and you love your kids, it'll work."

Carol Lavin Bernick, CEO, Polished Nickel Capital Management; Board member: Northwestern Memorial HealthCare, BDT Capital Partners Fund Advisory Committee, Executive Committee of the Chicago Community Trust; Author, *Gather as You Go*

"I love working. These days, I love helping the young ladies I mentor and sponsor. I'm all about leaving a legacy now, supporting the young women coming up behind us."

Sheila Robinson, Publisher and CEO, *Inclusion* and *Diversity Woman* magazines; Founder of Diversity Woman Media; Author, *Your Tool Kit for Success: The Professional Woman's Guide for Advancing in the C-Suite*

"Companies really need to adapt if they want to better support working families. They need to provide more flexible work arrangements, good maternity leave policies, childcare credits and really good managers. To women I say, if your boss isn't helping you be a working mom, then start looking for other options."

Carol Evans, CEO, Carol Evans Enterprises Inc.; Founder, President Emeritus, Working Mother Media, Diversity Best Practices, National Association for Female Executives; Co-Founder, Executive Women for Hillary/Her

The Likeability Dilemma (Mid-career Track)

Research suggests that there is a dilemma most women face in the professional world as they strive to build their careers – a choice between being perceived as competent or likeable. Both these qualities are of course imperative for success but as experts have reported, the incongruity of normative female roles (warm, nurturing) with characteristics perceived as necessary for professional success (independence, assertiveness) means that women are all too often perceived as likeable, but incompetent, or as competent, but unlikeable. Thus, if a woman pushes her team to perform or if she is decisive, she is deviating from the social script that dictates how she "should" behave. By violating those beliefs, successful women elicit pushback from others. As "B-word" descriptions like "Bullheaded" and "Ballbuster" can attest, today's U.S. culture seems deeply uncomfortable with powerful women. So, what's an aspiring female executive to do? Figuring out to what extent this is playing out in your workplace and what you personally can do to combat it is key to getting ahead.

Summary In 2003, Columbia Business school conducted research where students were asked to review a case study in which an entrepreneur started a company and over time made it very successful. The entrepreneur achieved this success through decisions that some people might find harsh – such as firing staff. Half of the students received a case study where the entrepreneur was a woman. For the other half, it was a man. The stories were identical aside from the entrepreneur's name and pronouns (Heidi vs Howard). However, when asked whether the fictional entrepreneur appeared trustworthy or likable, students consistently listed the female entrepreneur far below her male counterpart. The study was repeated in 2013 with similar results. This is an example of the likeability trap.

"I ran into this when I was promoted to brand manager. I was on an accelerated track. I was much younger than other brand managers and had people reporting to me that were not only older but more senior to me in the company. I got a lot of pushback. But I worked through it by quickly identifying people on my team who would support me and do good work for me. And by securing a very big, very visible win so that people could see us succeed. After that, everybody wanted to jump on the boat. And importantly, when they did, I welcomed them aboard."

Camiel J. Irving '14, Brand Manager, P&G Ventures

"I had a manager work for me once who said, 'It's so important when you're in a problem period to share little wins.' It brings up the team, it brings up morale and everybody likes everybody when they feel like they're winning. It helps you be seen both as competent and as a strong team leader."

Renee Weisman, Founder and Owner, Winning at Work; Author, *Winning in a Man's World: Advice for Women Who Want to Succeed and the Men Who Work With Them*

"I'd like to take the word likeable out of the equation. It's not about being likeable to me. It's about people wanting to work with you. And people are going to want to work with you if you have successes and you're competent and you're fun or you motivate them. Of course, I want to be nice every day. But I can't be. So, if a tough conversation goes wrong, I'm sure to circle back and have compassion when I do."

Cindi Bigelow '86, President & CEO, Bigelow Tea

"I work a lot with our first level managers— these are people who have recently been promoted and are now managing their first direct reports. Their pendulum is constantly swinging between being likeable and appearing competent and they don't know where to land. Consequently, they're often vague in how they manage. I tell them: You can't be everything to everybody. When you're managing, you have to figure out two things. One, who really matters? Who do I need to be my advocates? And two, what's your authentic brand of leadership?"

Sonali Lamba '12, Co-Founder, Brideside

"Lead with competence. Your competence is your credibility. That's what's going to get you your next promotion. That's what's going to get people to sing your praises in the hallways when you're not there. Should you think about and care about whether people like you? Sure. But you're being paid to do this job. So, be a likeable, kind person, but let that be 10 percent of your focus and let your competence be the other 90 percent."

Tarra Sharp '13, Engagement Manager, McKinsey & Company

Kellogg Connections Dinner

We've all done it. It's the end of a long day and all you want to do is get home or go back to the hotel and catch up on emails. But, that would be a mistake – one women make all too often. As any successful executive will tell you, relationship-building and networking are key to both succeeding where you are and landing that next coveted role.

This dinner focused on the power of connections, especially Kellogg connections. It featured two inspiring alumnae, Keech Combe Shetty '06 and Edith Cooper '86. Edith shared how relationships have been meaningful throughout her life and career and acknowledged how much the Global Women's Summit reinforced the power of connections between women.

Keech shared her personal story and spoke about a harrowing accident she experienced prior to starting at Kellogg. Her optimism, resilience and the support she received from her family, friends and Kellogg classmates made all the difference in her recovery. By telling their stories, Edith and Keech helped participants recognize how sharing our authentic selves with each other can create meaningful and lasting connections.

This session also challenged participants to put this new knowledge into practice by encouraging new connections between participants via lively table conversations focused on questions like:

1. What connections have been most meaningful to you?

2. How do you create and give advocacy?

3. How do you connect with people different than you?

4. How can you take action to build and deepen your connections?

5. How might you tap into Kellogg to help you and others?

Creating a Powerful Second Act

Are you ready to create a new, distinctly different career? Perhaps you have accomplished what you have set out to do over the years yet find yourself contemplating a new path. You may be closing a chapter and want to begin something new and are wondering what that will be and how to make that happen. This session featured a panel of women who created powerful second acts. Learn how they figured out their new direction, used their skills and experiences and positioned themselves for the next step.

Summary When you consider your professional journey, you'll likely find that your career has had multiple acts. Choosing your next step means tapping into your network to find the support and feedback necessary to help you think through the impact you want to have and where you want to have it.

"I had many good friends, other women CEOs, many of whom had gone through transitions, and I asked for their advice when I was transitioning. Of course, my family and I talked about it too. It had to work for all of us and it was a risk. When you're at Harley-Davidson and you're at the executive level making a lot of money, and then you're going off to start something new, how do you go through all those transitions in a way that you feel like you're supported?"

Donna F. Zarcone, President and CEO, The Economic Club of Chicago; Former President and COO, Harley-Davidson, Financial Services; Board member: Cigna Corporation, CDW and The Duchossois Group

"There are many important things to think about when you start looking for a life transition coach. What are you looking for? What kind of background do they have? I believe it's really important for a transition coach to have had a professional career. It's about chemistry, who you trust, who you respect, checking references, finding who you'll really work with. It's someone that can serve as a thought partner for you."

Gail R. Meneley, Co-Founder and Principal, Shields Meneley Partners

"When I left Whirlpool, I was looking to do good work with smart people. I wanted to get away from the bureaucracy, and I personally wanted to take a risk. I was at the 25-year mark with large companies but I felt like there was an entrepreneur inside me. I ended up becoming president of a small professional services firm and it gave me that element of risk-taking I'd always wanted. Later, when I came to Kellogg it was driven by wanting to make a difference. I wondered – what could I create that would be lasting?"

Ellen Taaffe '97, Clinical Assistant Professor of Leadership, Director of Women's Leadership Programs, Kellogg School of Management; Former executive, PepsiCo, Royal Caribbean and Whirlpool; Board member: John B. Sanfilippo & Son Inc., Hooker Furniture Corporation

"As I transitioned from corporate accounting to the YWCA, people were expecting me to say that I hated accounting and that I hated the corporate life. But that just wasn't the case. To me it was all about the possibilities of what the YWCA could be. When I came in we were an $11 million agency with a $1 million deficit. I thought too many people needed us to let this 140-year old organization die. I knew there were things that could be done differently. I became obsessed and that led me to throw my name in the hat. Five years later, we're a $23 million organization that is breaking even and growing tremendously."

Dorri McWhorter '09, CEO, YWCA Metropolitan Chicago; Former Partner, Crowe LLP

The Likeability Dilemma (Executive Track)

At a certain point on the way to the top, performance will no longer be enough. This is especially true for women and minorities. Too often, the very same hard-charging, "deliver against the odds" approach that many women take to get promoted from entry level to senior manager shifts from being an asset to a liability as they try to move into the C-suite or other executive roles. Why? Because on the top team, it is no longer enough to lead a single part of the organization, you must also be able to "play nice" with your peers while running the whole enterprise. At this juncture words like "fit" and "likeability" often take precedence over performance in the selection process. These words can be hard to define or defend against and they all too often take women out of the running. This reality can be disappointing, but it is manageable. So, the question is, how do you deal with it?

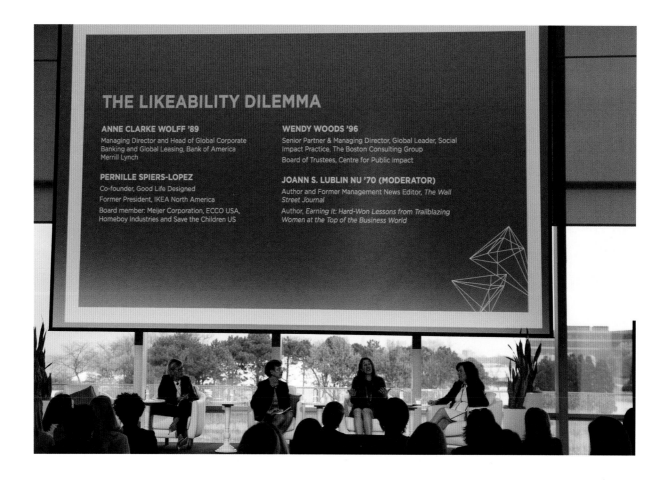

THE LIKEABILITY DILEMMA

ANNE CLARKE WOLFF '89
Managing Director and Head of Global Corporate Banking and Global Leasing, Bank of America Merrill Lynch

PERNILLE SPIERS-LOPEZ
Co-founder, Good Life Designed
Former President, IKEA North America
Board member: Meijer Corporation, ECCO USA, Homeboy Industries and Save the Children US

WENDY WOODS '96
Senior Partner & Managing Director, Global Leader, Social Impact Practice, The Boston Consulting Group
Board of Trustees, Centre for Public Impact

JOANN S. LUBLIN NU '70 (MODERATOR)
Author and Former Management News Editor, *The Wall Street Journal*
Author, *Earning It: Hard-Won Lessons from Trailblazing Women at the Top of the Business World*

"One woman I interviewed shared the isolation she often felt as the only woman in the room when ideas she had come up with were stolen by male colleagues. Since she wanted to be likeable, she didn't object. But then she also didn't get the credit. So, she devised a solution. In future meetings, she made sure she was not the only woman in the room. And, the two of them agreed ahead of time that if one saw the other's idea being overlooked, the other woman would jump in and say, 'Gosh! I'm really glad to hear you think so highly of her idea…' It worked. The proper person got the credit and neither woman's likeability suffered."

Joann S. Lublin NU '70, Author and Former Management News Editor, *The Wall Street Journal*; Author, *Earning It: Hard-Won Lessons from Trailblazing Women at the Top of the Business World*

"I've been told twice now that I'm not "likeable" but people always acknowledge my talent, my followership, the great things I can do with a business. I believe that women don't have to win because they're likeable. We can also win because we're effective."

Anne Clarke Wolff '89, Head of Global Corporate Banking and Global Leasing, Bank of America Merrill Lynch

"Will everybody like you? No. Is it okay that they don't? I had to be okay with that. If you're not okay with that you'll be an ineffective leader because someone will always be upset with you."

Pernille Spiers-Lopez, Co-Founder, Good Life Designed; Former President, IKEA North America; Board member: Meijer Corporation, ECCO USA, Homeboy Industries and Save the Children U.S.

"I try not to hinge on the word 'likeability' because that's giving someone else the power over me. What I focus on is how I want to be treated. I want to be treated with respect. I want people to listen to what I'm saying."

Wendy Woods '96, Senior Partner and Managing Director, Global Leader, Social Impact Practice, The Boston Consulting Group; Board member: Centre for Public Impact

Interacting Effectively with the Board

A very experienced director once said, "If I had gained some of my experience as a director when I was in my senior leadership role, I would have leveraged our company's board very differently. I always considered the board as a single entity I needed to manage and failed to see the individual expertise I could tap." How do you effectively leverage the expertise on your board and best manage your board interactions?

Summary Companies benefit from excellent interaction between the Board members and the senior management team and between the Board members themselves.

"You have to know your role. Be prepared. Anticipate questions. Know your audience. Less is often more with boards. We have to communicate with them crisply and succinctly. Be authentic and honest."

Diana Sands '96, Senior Vice President of the Office of Internal Governance and Administration and Member of the Executive Council, The Boeing Company

"I'd say it's important to help set the agenda for the CEO. But at the same time, be flexible within that agenda. What you think will happen won't always. Connected to that, you have to be able to read the room and understand how much each board member knows and understands. Some of them might have spent years in the industry but many of them haven't. It's about being flexible and knowing your audience."

Ilene S. Gordon, Executive Chairman, Ingredion Incorporated; Board member: Lockheed Martin and International Paper Company – Presiding Director

"The most effective interactions between management and a board are not when management is repeating everything the board members have already read in the charts they've been sent. It's hitting the tough issues and allowing a dialogue to take place. The most effective times are when the most senior leader in management has enough self-awareness that instead of trying to manage the board, they're trying to help the board understand and bring their questions to the forefront to create a more solid plan going forward."

Ellen Kullman '83, Co-Chair, Paradigm for Parity; Former Chair and CEO DuPont; Board member: United Technologies Corporation, Dell Technologies, Amgen, Goldman Sachs and Carbon3D

"Be brief. Be bright. Be gone."

Jan Fields, Former President, McDonald's USA; Board Member: Monsanto, Chico's FAS, Welbilt Inc. and Ronald McDonald House Charities

Positioning Yourself for a Board Seat

Many successful women long for a board role but are frustrated by the lack of opportunities. For a significant number, the final step to the boardroom feels elusive while for a handful of senior women, board offers seem to abound. Experienced directors generally say that the most challenging board seat to obtain is the first one, because it is difficult for sitting directors to assess how you will be as a director if you have never been one. What does it take to secure the first opportunity? How can you position yourself and leverage your network effectively to increase the likelihood of a board offer? Search firms claim that boards are actively seeking female directors, so why is your phone not ringing? This panel of experienced directors provides advice on how to secure a seat at the table and how to do the essential diligence on board opportunities to ensure that you want to sit at the table when you are invited.

Summary Kellogg has been helping women prepare for board opportunities for more than 15 years with the Women's Director Development Program. In that program we talk about the journey to the board room, including how to position yourself, finding a board that's the right fit and using your skill set to meet the needs of the organization.

GLOBAL WOMEN'S SUMMIT

"It's not like a job interview. In a job interview you have to be prepared and to make sure that you're highlighting your skill set. By the time you get to the board interview, they know who you are and they know what skills you're bringing. They are looking for fit and you want to make sure that's a part of what you're focused on, not pushing so hard on selling your skill set."

Victoria H. Medvec, Adeline Barry Davee Professor of Management and Organizations and Co-Founder and Executive Director, Kellogg Center for Executive Women, Kellogg School of Management

"An advisory board is a great way to get your foot in the door. You also make connections to potential investors and advisors, which can lead to other opportunities."

Patricia Riskind '97, CEO, Blue Horse Ventures; Board member: NarrativeDx, PatientWisdom, The Accreditation Council for Graduate Medical Education (ACGME) and Relode.com

"It's about the people. Because I've always felt, especially with board service, it's optional. Going on a board, you decide whether or not you want to be in the foxhole with that person. I always look at who those people are because my reputation is everything. I want to go on a board not only where I can contribute something, but I also always want to go on a board where I feel that I can get something back, like connections or people I want to be around."

Michele J. Hooper, CEO, The Directors' Council; Board member: PPG Industries, UnitedHealth Group, United Continental Holdings and the Smithsonian National Board

"Too often, they try to put us in a box. It blocks out so many other opportunities. You cannot sit in a dark room and think people are going to come after you. You have to figure out what it is that you can do that will make you happy and that you will genuinely be good at because you like to do it."

Jan Fields, Former President, McDonald's USA; Board Member: Monsanto, Chico's FAS, Welbilt Inc. and Ronald McDonald House Charities

Investing in Other Women Dinner

Melinda Gates recently noted, "The venture and startup ecosystem is still a boy's club – one that too often excludes, disadvantages and mistreats talented women who want to contribute to it." Overcoming this "boy's club" will require successful women to invest in female founders. Yet, many who have tried to raise funds from female investors find that women are risk-averse and slow to commit. Some women who have succeeded in their careers may not even know how to begin to make the transition to becoming an investor. Kellogg students are always taught about the importance of social capital, human capital and financial capital. This panel discussed how women can leverage their financial capital and use it to change the fate of the female founder.

Summary Women in the U.S. control $11.2 trillion of investable assets, and there could be as much as $5 billion in excess capital sitting on the sidelines. There is a tremendous opportunity for women to invest in female founders. It turns out that women who invest capital in women-owned businesses make invaluable contributions to the business, tend to be more engaged than male investors and earn significant returns.

"Women are underinvested in women. Less than 10 percent of venture capitalists are women. Less than eight percent of funding goes to gender-diverse founded teams and less than three percent to women entrepreneurs. And that has huge implications, not only for women wanting to start businesses, but also for the innovations we see in the world."

Andrea Turner Moffitt, Co-Founder and President, Plum Alley Investments; Author, *Harnessing the Power of the Purse: Winning Women Investors*

"There are people that can and don't and people that can and do. I always want to be on the 'do' side. So, just start. It's not that hard."

Linnea Conrad Roberts, Founder and CEO, GingerBread Capital; Former Managing Director, Goldman Sachs; Trustee, Roberts Foundation

"Women don't tend to pass the beer test. You meet with a VC group, you ace the Q&A and the investors lean back in their chairs and think, 'Do I want to go have a beer with this person after this investment?' The answer is, 'No!' We as women investors have a tremendous advantage in investing in women because we speak the same language and come from the same culture."

Sona Wang '86, Founder and Managing Director of the Ceres Venture Fund; Co-Founder, Chicago Blues Experience

"While their money was critical to the growth and success of our company, what I found was that my women investors were far more engaged with me and my team. They took a more vested interest in all sorts of issues. So, their value went way beyond a checkbook. It was opening doors, it was helping us recruit and interview talent. It's not just about the money. The value add behind the money is so critical."

Mary Naylor, Executive Chairman, Aspire Lifestyles Americas

"The value female investors have brought in terms of experience is invaluable. It's all about the fit and connection you can have with the investor, where you can have really important conversations. With male investors, they're very quick to tell you that you don't know what you're doing."

Bertha González Nieves NU '97. Co-Founder and CEO, Tequila Casa Dragones

CHAPTER 6

THE ROAD AHEAD

The slow progress of the last 40 years has shown us that achieving parity in the C-suite could take another 40 to 50 years. A half century, and that's if we're lucky. Without intervention, it could take longer – beyond 2100.

Research, personal experience and thousands of women's career journeys make clear: the challenge is not women's education, training or capabilities. It's the barriers that women continue to encounter on the way to C-suite, barriers that are complex and multifaceted. Overcoming them will require perseverance and a multi-stakeholder approach. It will require greater attention from companies and policy makers, as well as greater intention from the men and women in roles with the power to change women's trajectories. It will also require women themselves to take on the challenge of journeying further and harder.

Overcoming Resistance

We'll be honest. In doing this work, we've encountered some resistance. We've been asked many times why we chose to focus the book and the Summit on the road to the C-suite. Many of the women with whom we spoke during the process were quite clear: the C-suite is not their goal and they don't want to feel pressure to take it on. Many asked us to change or soften the frame.

We listened. We talked to many people. We reflected and we debated. We understood and understand the sentiment. It comes out of a desire to support *all* Kellogg women and our shared value of inclusivity. But in the end, we landed on the realization that if one of the world's great business schools, the *only* one thus far to be led by a woman,

publicly soft-peddles the goal of gender parity in the C-suite and the challenge of achieving it, we risk becoming part of the problem.

As we stated in the opening pages of this book, we recognize that the C-suite is not the final destination for all women – or men – who attend Kellogg. Nor should it be. But as a leading business school, we have an obligation to support, equip and propel any Kellogg woman who wants to aim there. We have to be a producer of C-suite leaders, regardless of gender.

To help understand this, we offer a sports analogy. Not all of our athletically gifted children can or want to be

Olympians. But this doesn't mean that, as parents, we don't want them to have the best training available. We do want to them learn discipline. We want them to learn focus. And, we want them to learn what best practices look like. With that preparation, the best and brightest will have options, including the option to pursue Olympic dreams, whether they always had them or they were awakened during the course of their development. The same holds true for how we prepare Kellogg leaders: we want them all to have options and to dream big.

Rising to the Challenge

Why are women disproportionately disengaging from the C-suite climb? The numbers make it clear: simply fixing the pipelines coming out of college and MBA programs does *not* fix the problem. Women have made up 50 percent or more of graduates from the nation's best undergraduate programs and 25 percent or more of graduates from the nation's best business schools for more than 20 years. Yet we have made little progress in increasing female representation in the C-suite, especially in the CEO position.

So we chose to lead Kellogg in stepping up. Effective leadership requires focus. We chose to focus on better preparing women for the C-suite, knowing that this will not just benefit how we educate women. It will benefit all Kellogg leaders, regardless of gender.

The pages of this book lay out the predictable pivot points that many women (and many men) encounter in building a business career: The Launch, The Mid-career Marathon and The Executive Transition. They also lay out the challenges that women face in each phase that are culturally and biologically different than those faced by their male peers.

To give each pivot point heft, we outlined the core development goals that women need to achieve in each phase of the journey. By outlining four dimensions of executive growth (people management, business knowledge, strategic thinking and relationship building) and demonstrating how they change across the pivot points, our goal was to add both richness and practical detail to help professional women better navigate their careers.

We believe these lessons and insights are valuable and applicable no matter where a woman ultimately chooses to take her career. And indeed, as we have seen with the Summit, the pivot points model and corresponding insights around executive growth are already having an impact.

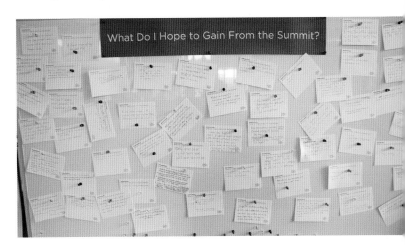

What Do I Hope to Gain From the Summit?

Providing a Roadmap for the Future

Below we offer a roadmap for the future, based on our research, our interviews and input from our Summit participants. We offer this roadmap in the form of an action list broken into two parts: what people must do and what organizations, including companies and Kellogg, must do.

This is not meant to be an all-inclusive action plan, and we recognize that many of our recommendations are well known. Nevertheless, if we deem them critical to progress, we've included them. It's worth noting that many of these recommendations will help not only women, but all voices that are underrepresented in the C-suite, including people of color, who this work has helped us see often face additional obstacles.

People

What men and women in positions of influence must do. First and foremost, progress will require that more people in positions of influence change their behavior. We each need to take responsibility every day for our words and our actions. Every senior leader, every professor, every career coach who works with rising executives has the opportunity to make a difference in words and deeds. We each need to be willing and able to ask ourselves: what am I doing to improve the situation for women (or not)?

The basics include:

- Get training on unconscious bias.

- Be a role model in how and how often we affirm and productively engage female colleagues in meetings and in hallways.

- Seek to publicly affirm women's leadership contributions when we communicate in public forums (speeches, blogs, etc.).

- Make it a goal to formally coach and mentor at least one more woman each year than we do now.

- Require that at least one woman be considered for every new hire, promotion and board appointment decision in which we participate.

- Be intentional about executive development for high-potential women (and men) starting in their mid-thirties. Track people's progress; get them all coaching, balance out how they each develop their skillsets over time.

What family and friends can do. It's well documented that how children are raised influences the choices they make as adults. And, how adults are supported by those around them affects their confidence, motivations and sense of well-being. If we want more women leading, we need to:

- Raise daughters who want to lead.
  - Introduce our daughters to role models and stories that support and integrate femininity and family with ambition and agency.
  - Watch our language. When a young girl exhibits self-advocacy, self-agency or willfulness, call her a self-starter, a problem-solver, a team advocate, a leader. Even if she's being annoying, affirm what's good about what she is doing, then teach her how to finesse it.
  - Teach our daughters how to build teams with boys in sports, in household chores and in lemonade stands.
  - Teach our daughters to keep raising their hands, literally and figuratively, and to effectively use the airtime and access they get.
  - Teach our daughters to model inclusivity with other women. Actively discourage "queen bee" attitudes and the desire to build exclusive cliques during the middle- and high-school years. Affirm your daughter for fostering a diverse group of friends.

- Raise sons who enjoy teaming with girls.
  - Teach our sons how to cook, grocery shop, manage a household and do dishes and laundry.
  - Coach our sons to want girls to be part of the team in the robotics

lab, on the playing field and during community service.

- Equip our sons with language that admires character and strength in girls. Banish language that puts women in an inferior position, e.g., "you throw like a girl."
- Introduce our sons to female role models who integrate femininity and family with ambition and agency.

• Encourage young women to launch well in their twenties, to take stretch jobs and not seek comfort and balance before their careers even get started.

• Help mid-career women – our sisters, female colleagues or friends – stay in the workforce full-time and thrive. Help can come in innumerable ways, from being a good listener to a back-up babysitter to a carpool partner.

• Encourage and support executive women who decide to take on the C-suite challenge. Be a sounding board, send encouraging notes, invite them to get-togethers (even knowing they may have to cancel), thank them for being role models, write stories that laud their accomplishments. It may not be for everyone, but keep in mind that those women who do decide to go for it aren't just doing it for themselves. Their success lifts us all.

What women must do for themselves.
No matter what their destination, ambitious women need to be intentional as they build their careers. To do this, they need to anticipate each pivot point and its unique challenges. Specifically, we believe women need to:

• Understand how executive growth is achieved over time in order to make smart choices about their own development. Each woman needs to be thoughtful about when and how to seek out new opportunities and

ask for stretch assignments. She also needs to be reflective about her own progress.

- Build professional support networks, similar to YPO groups, especially during the mid-career years, in which a group of high-potential women commit to staying connected and accountable as they weather career challenges.

- Consider hiring a career coach, using their own money if need be, to help with executive development and round out skill sets.

- Think through all possible options before completely stepping out of the workforce during The Mid-career Marathon, making that choice the last resort. And if they must step out,

try not to do so for longer than 12 months.

- Work hard to find part-time employment that keeps skills relevant if slowing down during The Mid-career Marathon is necessary. Though part-time work may add stress in the short run, it will provide better options longer term, especially after children have left home.

- Consider asking for a sabbatical versus quitting if the years of hard work catch up at The Executive Transition point. We've found that many companies will work with proven executives in order to shore them up for a continued run into their fifties and beyond. Sometimes, even for women who feel they've had enough, a real break is all that is needed to refuel or address a pressing personal issue.

- Go for it if asked to join the C-suite. Even just a couple of years in the C-suite can make a big difference – to other women through role modeling, to organizations through changing organizational norms and frankly, to the women themselves, as it significantly increases option value when they later step down.

Organizations

What companies must do. We've reached a point where it's both a moral and business imperative that companies employ the best available talent, regardless of gender, ethnicity or socio-economic background. Here are some actions that have been shown to make a difference in hiring *and* retaining more diverse talent and realizing the value of increased diversity.

Hiring practices

- Embrace gender-neutral hiring. This includes setting position salaries in advance – not based on prior salary history – and removing names and addresses from initial screenings.

- Mandate diverse, balanced slates for every role and publicly post job openings, so everyone has an equal chance to raise their hands.

- Revise job descriptions to be broader (versus overly task specific), as women tend not to apply for roles if they perceive they are missing a specific qualification.

- Mandate diverse interview panels to review each candidate for new hires and promotions.

- Implement and publicly track targets for diversity (not just women) at every level and report progress annually.

Building culture

- Use language and enact policies that aren't biased for or against anyone.

- Provide repeated training on unconscious bias for everyone. As it's *un*conscious, it takes time to truly increase awareness and understanding.

- Evaluate top leaders annually on tangible, inclusive behavior metrics.

- Celebrate leaders at all levels who have track records of hiring and developing diverse talent and fostering diverse teams.

- Celebrate leaders at all levels who represent diversity and have successfully challenged the organization to become more inclusive.

Mid-career support resources

- Create, sponsor and publicly affirm mid-career resource groups to assure that the best women (and men) are really supporting each other through the marathon years.

- Provide formal coaching for all high-potential women (and men), especially as they enter the thick of the mid-career years, to provide timely feedback and facilitate more focus on their development as well as minimize the chances of a complete exit.

- Offer more flexible schedules where possible, including at least some C-suite feeder roles.

- Offer re-boarding programs that specifically seek out qualified candidates looking to re-join the workforce or rejoin the organization (sometimes referred to as boomerang programs).

- As has been frequently cited, provide more on-site childcare or invest in high-quality childcare providers located near work sites. It's not new, but it works. Families still need more high-quality, affordable options.

C-suite review

- Examine the C-suite, C-suite minus one and C-suite minus two ranks – How many women (and other diverse employees) are there? Are there enough? If not, is it clear why?

- Hire an outside firm to confidentially interview all women (and other diverse employees) who have exited the company over the last three years who were within three rungs of the C-suite (e.g., usually senior directors and above), to hear directly and discretely about why they left.

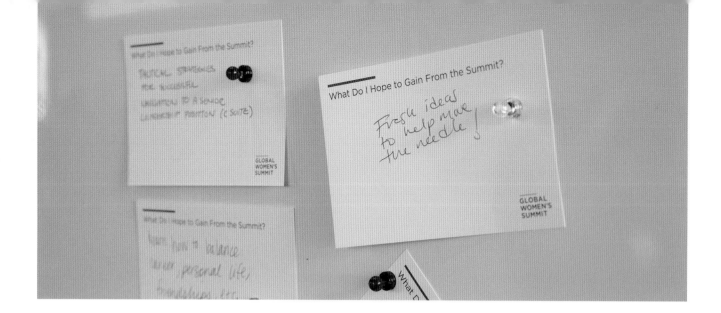

- Mandate confidential, senior-level exit interviews going forward for *all* diverse leaders leaving within three rungs of the C-suite; have these scheduled confidentially and off-site. Be sure the unvarnished findings are reported to the executive team and the board of directors.

- Consider developing formal options for high-potential senior executives in their mid-forties to early fifties to get a three- to six-month sabbatical, paid or unpaid, as a means of recharging. We met several high performers, both male and female, who took one, found it transformational and have been running at full steam ever since.

What Kellogg can do. Last but not least, there are more things that Kellogg can do and do better. Before we list them, it's important to note that as a business school, we are designed and funded to educate tuition-paying students and conduct research. Within that sphere, we commit to endeavor to:

Build out leadership programming for our female students.

- Deepen the content and impact of our co-curricular Women's Leadership Seminar for our full-time female students.

- Develop and deliver women's leadership programming tailored to meet the needs of female students in our evening/weekend and EMBA programs.

- Convene events that celebrate, connect and catalyze our female students.

Enhance our curricular offerings.

- Lead the field in developing better language and distinct content around a) hiring, retaining and developing diverse talent, and b) building teams, cultures and companies that include, embrace and benefit from diverse perspectives, whether that diversity comes from demographic differences, personality differences or expertise differences.

- Require training for all students on unconscious bias, managing diversity and developing inclusive leadership practices.

- Expand and integrate formal course offerings for all degree programs on hiring, retaining and developing diverse talent and building inclusive teams, cultures and companies.

Build out our Open Doors initiative.

- Make Kellogg ever more diverse within and among our student, faculty and staff communities. Set targets and hold ourselves accountable for progress.

- Make the Kellogg culture best in class on including and embracing difference within and among our students, faculty and staff.
  - Conduct formal culture reviews within each degree program, academic department and operating unit to gauge how different voices are feeling heard and represented.
  - Provide training on inclusive leadership for our faculty and staff in each degree program, academic department and operating unit, as well as for our student and alumni leaders.
  - Set goals and appoint resource leaders within each degree program, academic department and operating unit to improve inclusion metrics.

Deploy our alumni team.

- Guide our alumnae in expanding the agenda and impact of The Kellogg Executive Women's Network (KEWN) in Chicago.

- Support our alumnae in building KEWN chapters in other major markets.

- Encourage all alumni clubs to provide alumnae programming that taps into the expertise of local alumnae and female business leaders.

- Plan the timing and content for future convenings of Kellogg alumnae.

Deploy our executive education team.

- Identify executive education program opportunities (and accompanying funding models) to support and develop female executives during the mid-career years.

- Enhance and expand programming offered for senior women through the Kellogg Center for Executive Women.

- Elevate the awareness and impact of our registry of board-ready Women's Director Development Program graduates.

CODA

At Kellogg, our purpose is to educate, equip and inspire brave leaders who build strong organizations and wisely leverage the power of markets to create lasting value.

If we believe that achieving gender parity in the C-suite will make our companies, our society and our world stronger and wiser, we need to bravely take on the challenge of making that happen.

If not us, then who?

CONTRIBUTORS

Cindi Bigelow '86
Third-Generation President & CEO, Bigelow Tea

Family-owned Bigelow Tea is a U.S. specialty tea market leader that produces two billion teabags annually. Cindi Bigelow holds a BS degree from Boston College, an MBA from Kellogg, as well as honorary doctorates from Fairfield University and the University of New Haven. She frequently makes appearances sharing insights on business ethics and career development, and has received numerous awards for her community service. Her pastimes include travel, skiing, tennis, yoga and drinking lots of Bigelow tea.

"Enjoy every single minute of your Kellogg experience. What you will take away from Kellogg is so much more than just what you learn in the classroom. I truly believe what you are exposed to over your two years will stay with you a lifetime, so make sure you appreciate everything happening around you from the minute you walk onto the campus."

Suzanne Blaug '83
Senior Vice President, Global Marketing and Commercial Development, Amgen

Suzanne Blaug is responsible for providing commercial leadership for Amgen products at all stages of the product life cycle and for maximizing value across the portfolio. Prior to joining Amgen in 2012, Suzanne spent eight years at Johnson & Johnson, where she was the head of a late-stage R&D company, as well as Vice President, Strategic Marketing at Janssen EMEA. She joined J&J in 2004 as Area Managing Director in Europe.

"Kellogg exposed me to people I never would have been exposed to otherwise. It was probably the first time I understood that there was a lot to learn from people who are very different from me."

Roslyn M. Brock '99
Chairman Emeritus, National Board of Directors, NAACP and
Vice President, Advocacy and Government Relations, Bon Secours Health System Inc.

Roslyn M. Brock is a prominent health and social justice leader, noted public speaker and ordained minister. Her 30-plus years of experience includes health care policy and health equity analysis, social justice advocacy, philanthropy and youth leadership development. She holds positions on the Kellogg Global Advisory Board, the Board of Trustees at George Washington University, and on the boards of the National NAACP and the Interfaith Center on Corporate Responsibility. Her trademark motto is "Courage will not skip this generation."

"Absorb everything you can from Kellogg. Speak with the professors and with the dean. Take the time to really get to know your teammates and others in your class. You will find that relationships are primary, all else is derivative."

Anne Clarke Wolff '89
Head of Global Corporate Banking and Global Leasing, Bank of America Merrill Lynch

Anne Clarke Wolff is managing director and head of Global Corporate Banking and Global Leasing at Bank of America Merrill Lynch. She is responsible for the firm's corporate banking coverage efforts globally. She additionally leads the country's largest equipment leasing company. She holds a BA from Colby College and an MBA from Kellogg. She currently serves on the boards of The Public Theater and the Brooklyn Historical Society and is a Trustee of Colby College. She was recently named to the board of directors of Amphenol Corporation.

"You can always tell somebody who went to Kellogg. Other schools have team projects, but Kellogg has the more elegant way of making that teamwork part of the DNA."

Keech Combe Shetty '06

Co-CEO, Combe Inc.

Keech Combe Shetty is a third generation leader of Combe Inc. Her family began the firm with Clearasil in 1949; today it is a global company with brands like Just For Men and Vagisil. She serves on the Board of Directors for Combe Inc., the Personal Care Products Council, the Edna Adan Hospital Foundation and the Consumer Healthcare Products Association. Keech holds an MBA from Kellogg and a BA in political science and international studies from Northwestern.

"One of things that originally attracted me to Kellogg was the family enterprise program. Kellogg's John Ward is the 'godfather' of family enterprise. Having someone understand, from a professional point of view, the concept of a family business and how it combines business with almost family counseling was key. I'd never experienced anything like that before in my life."

Edith Cooper '86

Former Partner and Global Head of Human Capital Management. Goldman Sachs and Board of Directors, Etsy and Slack Technologies, Inc.

During her time at Goldman Sachs, Edith Cooper was responsible for the recruitment, development, promotion and well-being of the firm's 35,000 employees around the world. Prior to this role, she worked in Sales Management and led several businesses within the firm's Securities Division. She serves on the Board of Trustees of the Museum of Modern Art as well as the Board of Trustees at Northwestern. She is also a member of the Boards of Directors of Horizons at Brunswick School and ExpandED Schools.

"Once you've received your degree, you will be launching into the next set of relationships that you will have with Kellogg. I graduated in 1986 and 20 years went by before I had any further connection with the University. Kellogg's leadership recognized that it was important to reach out to a broader group of alums to get input on the direction of the school's mission. I have benefited from this reengagement — benefited as a professional, as part of a community of professionals and as a senior woman."

Ann Drake '84
Chairman & CEO, DSC Logistics Inc.

In addition to leading DSC Logistics, Ann Drake is a member of the Kellogg Global Advisory Board, the Board of Governors for Chicago's Metropolitan Planning Council and the Board of Trustees for Chicago's Museum of Science and Industry. She is also the recipient of numerous awards and accolades, including the Council of Supply Chain Management Professionals Distinguished Service Award, the global Women Who Make a Difference Award from the International Women's Forum and the Schultz Award from the McCormick School of Engineering at Northwestern. She is the founder of AWESOME and a charter member of Paradigm for Parity.

"For a young woman starting Kellogg today, I think the most important thing is to be confident, so do whatever you can to develop that confidence at Kellogg. And practice saying 'yes' when opportunities arise."

Lisa Earnhardt '96
President & CEO, Intersect ENT

Lisa Earnhardt leads Intersect ENT, a medical technology company dedicated to improving the quality of life for patients with ear, nose and throat conditions. Lisa has more than two decades of healthcare experience. She serves on the boards of Intersect ENT, Nevro, AdvaMed and the Kellogg Global Advisory Board. She received a Bachelor of Science in industrial engineering from Stanford University and an MBA from Kellogg.

"What's really unique at Kellogg is the spirit of teamwork and collaboration. I'm such a huge believer in the power of collaboration. All the late nights and weekends you spend in group meetings, working through challenges, that's actually when so much of the learning happens."

Kathy Elsesser '93
Global Chair of the Healthcare Group and Consumer and Retail Group,
Goldman Sachs

Kathy Elsesser is Global Chair of the Healthcare Group and Consumer and Retail Group in the Investment Banking Division at Goldman Sachs and serves as a member of the IBD Executive Committee. Kathy joined Goldman Sachs in 1989 as a financial analyst and rejoined the firm in 1993 as an associate after graduating from Kellogg. She was named Managing Director in 2002 and Partner in 2004. She lives in Brooklyn with her husband and three children and serves on a number of non-profit boards.

"I think women completely undervalue how good the accounting and finance classes are at Kellogg. Because of that, they shy away from them. But Kellogg women can be hugely successful in jobs that are often seen to be male dominated."

Ashleigh Gibson '13
Associate Director, Brand Building, The Kraft Heinz Company

Ashleigh Gibson is an Associate Director at the Kraft Heinz Company. She oversees strategy, innovation and communications development for frozen foods. Ashleigh joined KHC after graduating from Kellogg. Prior to KHC, Ashleigh worked in start-up nonprofit organizations that created pipelines for talented, underrepresented minorities in NYC. There she led strategic programs, marketing and fundraising. In 2007, Ashleigh graduated summa cum laude with a B.S. in Journalism from Oklahoma State University.

"A lot of other schools are great at making people good managers. Kellogg has the ability to transform people into incredible leaders."

Vinita Gupta '92

CEO, Lupin Limited

Vinita Gupta is a graduate in pharmacy from the University of Mumbai. She has not only been responsible for starting Lupin's business in the U.S, now the largest part of the company, but has also been instrumental in formulating and executing the strategies that have helped the company emerge as a global pharmaceutical powerhouse and one of the most exciting growth stories in the pharmaceutical industry.

"Before Kellogg, I had lived in a very protective environment in India. Kellogg gave me the exposure I needed to gain a global perspective. Its expertise in marketing and international business was exactly the training I needed to globalize the company."

Betsy D. Holden '82

Senior Advisor, McKinsey & Company and Former Co-CEO, Kraft Foods Inc.

Betsy D. Holden has been both CEO of the largest food company in North America and a strategy and marketing consultant. She broke barriers as one of the first female CEOs of a major company and is a champion for women in the workplace. She has been named one of *Fortune*'s Most Powerful Women multiple times and was inducted into the Chicago Business Hall of Fame. Betsy serves on the Kellogg Global Advisory Board, on the boards of Dentsply Sirona, Diageo plc and Western Union, plus the boards of multiple nonprofits.

"Kellogg provides an incredible opportunity to continue to identify your passions and refine what you're good at. There are so many opportunities to lead, to develop you and to build relationships. I've gotten so much value and fulfillment from making Kellogg a lifelong connection. I have come back here every year to recruit, to teach, to mentor. I've stayed in touch with my professors. I've invested in and gotten so much from the broader network."

Barbara B. Hulit '91
Senior Vice President, Fortive Corporation

Barbara B. Hulit is responsible for the Fortive Business System Office, High-Growth Markets and IT, bringing a commitment to innovation to these functions. Previously, she was with Danaher, where she successfully ran a $1 billion+ business. After Kellogg, Barbara became a partner with The Boston Consulting Group and led the Global Packaged Goods practice. Passionate about education, she serves on the Kellogg Global Advisory Board and the boards of the Pacific Science Center and the Washington Roundtable.

"Take advantage of the community in front of you. There's no other time in your life where you're going to have 100 companies that might be interested in talking to you about working for them. There's no other time in your life where you're going to have great professors who have done tremendous research and know such amazing case studies about what's happened in the real world. There's no other time where you're going to have hundreds of peers who are in a collaborative setting that lets you look under the tent and see what's really going on."

Camiel J. Irving '14
Brand Manager, P&G Ventures

Camiel J. Irving is a brand builder and corporate entrepreneur. She joined Procter & Gamble in 2014 after completing her MBA, and was quickly promoted into P&G Ventures, the company's new brand accelerator. At P&G Ventures, Camiel is leading P&G's entrance into the Menopause Care category. Outside the office, she is working on a household needs start-up; she also volunteers at her church, practices yoga and enjoys traveling the world with friends.

"I was offered a full ride to another business school and I turned it down to go to Kellogg because I felt like I belonged there. It was the best bet I ever made on myself, and it's paid out in multiples. Kellogg introduced me to some of my closest friends. My professional network is filled with people I genuinely love. At Kellogg I learned to lead with passion, empathy and fearlessness."

Ellen Kullman '83
Former Chair & CEO, DuPont and Co-Chair, Paradigm for Parity

During her seven years as CEO, Ellen Kullman guided DuPont through the global financial crisis of 2008 and transformed the company by exiting commoditized businesses and establishing DuPont as a premier, market-driven science company. She is a member of the boards of directors of United Technologies Corporation, Dell Technologies, Amgen, Goldman Sachs and Carbon 3D. She is also a member of the National Academy of Engineering and past chair of the US-China Business Council. She serves on the Board of Trustees for Northwestern and the board of overseers of Tufts School of Engineering.

"Women entering Kellogg today probably have a preconceived notion of what they want to get out of it. But I think they should open their minds. I think they should explore all of what Kellogg has to offer and only then chart their course. "

Sonali Lamba '12
Co-Founder & COO, Brideside

Sonali Lamba is the Co-Founder and COO of Brideside, an omni-channel retailer that has reimagined the way women shop for weddings and other meaningful moments in life. Sonali oversees the company's technology, merchandise and product strategy, customer experience and general operations. Sonali met her co-founder during orientation at Kellogg. She lives in Chicago with her husband and daughter.

"When I came to Kellogg, I made a choice not to belong to the women's business association. I didn't think that I needed to. And no one scolded me for not joining the WBA. Now I wish someone had. Dealing with male investors in a male-dominated industry, I wish that I knew more about the challenges I was going to face as a female business owner and a female business leader. This is entirely on me. I take responsibility for it. But, I don't want any other women going to Kellogg to have the same fate."

Jenny Lee '01

Managing Partner, GGV Capital

Jenny Lee is a global venture capitalist who works with young founders in China and the U.S. to create innovation through technology. Ranked seven consecutive times on *Forbes'* Global 100 VC Midas List, Jenny is recognized as a product-centric investor who enjoys discussing disruptive trends with her entrepreneurs. She firmly believes that a single person's vision, passion, creativity and grit, combined with the right capital, can create businesses and products to better the world.

"Business today is global. So, having participants from different regions, whether from Southeast Asia or South America, and learning how to accommodate different languages and different learnings is extremely valuable. Kellogg can help you learn that."

Kathleen L. McGinn '92

Cahners-Rabb Professor Business Administration, Harvard Business School, Harvard University

Kathleen L. McGinn studies gender at work, at home and in negotiations, in families across 29 countries, within communities in India, among women "firsts" in North America and among young women in Zambia. She served as Harvard Business School's Senior Associate Dean for Faculty Development, Director of Research and Chair of Doctoral Programs. She advises firms on gender and inclusion and serves on the boards of CFK Inc. (U.S. and Kenya) and WAVE (U.S. and Nigeria).

"The thing I couldn't have gotten anywhere else was my advisors. They were amazing. I was older than my fellow students and had already had a career. Toward the end of my second semester, my advisor said, 'You need to start teaching.' It wasn't the norm and if my advisor hadn't been paying attention to me as a person as well as a scholar, I could've been miserable."

Diana L. Nelson '89
Board Chair, Carlson

Diana L. Nelson is the Board Chair of Carlson, a privately held company that in its 80-year history has owned and operated global travel and hospitality businesses that include Carlson Wagonlit Travel, the world's largest travel management company. Diana is a magna cum laude graduate of Harvard College and received her MM from the Kellogg School of Management in 1989. She has extensive governance experience on both corporate and charitable boards. Diana and her husband, John Atwater, have five children and reside in San Francisco.

"Kellogg has a true heritage in integrative decision-making and collaborative approaches. Other schools have copied group work, but I still believe Kellogg is different and continues to push along those dimensions."

Wendy Nelson '99
Chair, Carlson Family Foundation & Board of Directors, Carlson

Wendy Nelson currently holds several governance roles within Carlson. She is the first in the Carlson family's third generation to be elected to Chair the Carlson Family Foundation. She began her career as a professional tennis player before transitioning to the corporate sector. Ten years ago, she shifted from management to governance, focusing on leadership and organizations that create equity, access and opportunity. Her current board service spans the for-profit and nonprofit sectors and proudly includes a place on the Board of Trustees for Northwestern.

"The true gift of Kellogg is the people you engage with during the journey to a degree. Kellogg is unique because of the class curation. The unique lens by which they select the individuals in each class to ensure the experience is rich with diversity on every level, from race to gender to nationality to experience set. From musicians to military veterans. This opportunity to listen, learn and explore with diverse voices creates a foundation to succeed and lead in a global marketplace — to lead in the world we live in today."

Efrat Peled '04
Chairman & CEO, Arison Investments

Efrat Peled is Chairman and CEO of Arison Investments, and leads the Shari Arison Family Office, estimated at a combined asset value in excess of $6 billion. She sits on several major industrial and philanthropic boards. Efrat is a former member of the World Economic Forum's Young Global Leaders and the Clinton Global Initiative Lead Group. She is repeatedly ranked in *Fortune*'s 50 Most Powerful Women in Business and on *Forbes'* World's 100 Most Powerful Women. Efrat was honored with the Northwestern University Alumni Merit Award.

"I decided to do the Kellogg executive MBA program because I wanted something out of the box. Kellogg was fairly new to Israel and joint international programs were fairly new concepts. The exposure to different cultures, different people and the fact we needed to work in teams was transformational for me. It gave me amazing tools that I definitely couldn't get from any other program in Israel. From a global perspective, Kellogg is really leading on these topics."

Paula B. Pretlow '78
Former Senior Vice President, The Capital Group

Born and raised in Oklahoma City, Paula B. Pretlow has made the San Francisco Bay Area home since graduating from Kellogg. She has spent her entire career in finance, most recently as a Senior Vice President at the Capital Group. Passionate about service and impact, Paula serves on for-profit and foundation boards that include the CION Ares Diversified Credit Fund, the Kresge Foundation and the Harry & Jeanette Weinberg Foundation. She is the proud mother of Neil (wife, Tanya) and Alison.

"Drink from the firehose. Discover your passion. Go toward it. Be all that you can be and do all that you can do. If you do this, when you come out, you'll be well equipped to pursue your dreams."

Jana Schreuder '83
COO, The Northern Trust Company

During the past 38 years, Jana Schreuder has held a variety of roles: President of Wealth Management, Chief Risk Officer, eCommerce Director, President for Operations & Technology and CEO of Northern Trust Retirement Consulting. Her leadership development focuses on learning from fellow directors of public, private and nonprofit boards. Most important, she and her husband of 39 years are proud parents of a daughter just beginning her own professional journey.

"Kellogg very quickly gave me the grounding I needed in core business functions. That quickly built my confidence, which was key as I had started working with bankers and people who had come from the credit training program and really understood business fundamentals."

Tarra Sharp '13
Engagement Manager, McKinsey & Company

Tarra Sharp is an Engagement Manager at McKinsey & Company. Previously, she worked in marketing at Citi Cards, American Express and American Airlines. She holds an MBA from Kellogg with concentrations in Strategy & Management and Entrepreneurship, and a BBA in Marketing from Baylor University. She sits on the boards of the Evening Associates-Art Institute of Chicago and Open the Circle. She lives in Chicago with her husband, Evan, and dog, Kofi.

"There's a real concern for other people in the Kellogg culture. There's a feeling that someone else's success doesn't mean you're missing out. I'm not sure that happens at other business schools."

Nicole Staple '12
Co-Founder & CEO, Brideside

Nicole Staple is the co-founder and CEO of Brideside. She runs all finance and revenue-generating operations, including sales, marketing and capital raising. Prior to founding Brideside, Nicole spent four years in healthcare investment banking and technology venture capital, where she supported large M&A transactions and growth investments. She holds a MBA from Kellogg, where she was awarded The Women's Business Association Scholarship, and a Bachelor of Arts degree in Economics from Wellesley College.

"I don't know if Brideside would have been the path I would have taken, had we not started it in school. The headspace and support from our class and professors was critical. We took this concept through many classes and many Kellogg classmates touched this business. Priceless."

Alice M. Tybout '75
Harold T. Martin Professor of Marketing, Kellogg School of Management, Northwestern University

Alice M. Tybout joined the Kellogg Marketing faculty upon completing her PhD at Northwestern in 1975. She has served as chairperson of the Marketing Department, won multiple teaching awards and co-edited two books: *Kellogg on Branding* and *Kellogg on Marketing* (second edition). She is also widely published in scholarly journals. Her contributions to the field of consumer research were recognized when she was made a Fellow of the Association for Consumer Research in 2016.

"Kellogg has created a global network that is priceless. No matter where I go around the globe, there's always a Kellogg connection. Sometimes the connection is with good friends made during my years at Kellogg, other times its with strangers who are happy to meet and open doors because we have Kellogg in common. Kellogg creates a family that bridges distances and cultures. Invest in and use these connections to help you, personally and professionally."

Wendy Woods '96

Senior Partner & Managing Director, Global Leader, Social Impact Practice,
The Boston Consulting Group (BCG)

Wendy Woods, Senior Partner and Managing Director, leads BCG's Social Impact Practice. She works with businesses, governments and social sector organizations to improve global health, development, education, the environment, humanitarian response, total societal impact and impact investing. She helps clients rethink business's role in society, create inclusive strategies and partnerships, improve effectiveness and drive change. She has given two TED talks: "The Business Benefits of Doing Good" and "Collective Cooperation in the Social Sector."

"When I think about the world today, the range of capabilities needed to solve any social issue is vast and diversity of thought is incredibly important. What I got from Kellogg was confidence in my problem-solving abilities, a diverse network and lifelong friends."

WELCOM

AUTHORS

Sally Blount '92

Sally Blount is an internationally recognized thought leader in management and business education. She is currently the The Michael L. Nemmers Professor of Strategy at the Kellogg School of Management at Northwestern University, where she teaches courses on leadership and organizational transformation.

From 2010–2018, she served as dean at Kellogg and, from 2004–2010, as dean of the Undergraduate College at New York University's Stern School of Business. A glass ceiling breaker at both schools, Blount was the first woman to be appointed dean at any U.S. or global top-10 business school. In 2017, she was recognized by LinkedIn as one of the Top Voices and by *Poets&Quants* as business school Dean of the Year. Blount sits on two Fortune 500 and several not-for-profit boards and is regularly featured in news outlets such as *The Wall Street Journal*, *Financial Times*, *Forbes*, *The Economist*, *Bloomberg Businessweek*, *Fortune* and MSNBC.

Perry Yeatman

Perry built her career making bold moves across a variety of sectors (business, government, philanthropy and education), disciplines (from Corporate Affairs to General Management), and nations (100+) as a senior executive at Kraft Foods, Unilever and Burson-Marsteller.

She has been a passionate advocate for working women, speaking at events including the World Economic Forum, The Conference Board and The U.S. Chamber of Commerce and contributing to a variety of media, including *Fortune*, *Forbes* and *The Huffington Post*. She is also co-author of the award-winning book *Get Ahead by Going Abroad: A Women's Guide to Fast-Track Career Success* (Harper Collins, 2007).

More recently, Perry founded the strategic consulting firm, Perry Yeatman Global Partners, and Your Career, Your Terms®, a social enterprise dedicated to providing women with the insights and inspiration they need to succeed. Through her companies, she continues to advise C-suite executives and not-for-profit institutions, including the Kellogg School of Management.

ACKNOWLEDGMENTS

First and foremost, my thanks to Kellogg – past, present and future. Three big shout-outs to Don Jacobs, Max Bazerman and Maggie Neale. Who would have known that the decision to attend Kellogg in 1988 would have been so formative? I am grateful for three decades of deeply meaningful work, a rich family life as mother to Missy and my Kellogg-born babies Haley and Cameron, and a wonderful global tapestry of dear family members and friends. My thanks to Perry for catalyzing me to put our "women's work" into book form and assure that we, and Kellogg, said something distinct. And last but not least, I thank and dedicate my work on this book to the memory of my mom, Mary Jane Blount, the woman who taught me how to dream.

– Sally

Professionally, my first thanks have to go to Sally and the Kellogg team who welcomed me into their wonderful community more than five years ago. You have expanded my thinking, allowed me to do world-class work and made me better in so many ways. I'll forever be grateful. I also want to thank the numerous women – and men – who believed in and supported me on my career journey. I simply couldn't have made it without your help and guidance. Personally, I want to thank my husband, Christian, my family and my friends, all of whom have had my back through numerous relocations and career transitions. Last but certainly not least, I dedicate my work on this book to my daughter and stepson. I urge you both to chase your dreams as passionately as I have chased mine. Andre, I wish you much success as you launch your career. I look forward to watching you become the fully-inclusive, high-impact business executive

I know you can be. Kirsten, you bring me such joy and inspire me to be my best self. I hope you will be equally inspired by the incredible women in this book and your mom who helped bring their stories and insights to light.

– Perry

We also want to thank those whose efforts contributed in so many ways to the inaugural Global Women's Summit, and to the book you hold in your hands, including:

- The more than 50 Summit Steering Committee members, especially, the co-chairs: Edith Cooper, Ilene Gordon and Ellen Kullman;
- The Global Women's Summit Faculty Advisory Committee members, including chair Victoria Medvec, and Bernard Banks, Kathleen Hagerty, Julie Hennessy, Lauren Rivera, Paola Sapienza, and Nicole Stephens;
- The rest of the Global Women's Summit planning co-chairs, Diana Cordova, Wendy Kritt, Victoria Medvec and Ellen Taaffe;
- The Alumnae we interviewed and those who participated in the global alumni survey;
- The Kellogg team who assisted in developing, implementing and analyzing the alumni survey, including Krista Edlund Gallagher and Nicole Stephens;
- The Kellogg faculty and staff who reviewed our manuscript, most especially Marni Futterman, Tom Hubbard, Jessica Love and Holly Raider;
- The Kellogg advancement team, especially Lisa Guynn and Ragan Royal;
- All the Kellogg workstream teams who helped ensure the Summit went off without a hitch, including Impact and Practice, External Relations, Creative and Digital Services, Information Services and Facilities;
- The Dean's office staff, including Julie Dahlinger, Arlene Johnson, Emma Valind and Cassandra Wallace;
- Those companies and organizations that shared their research, including Accenture, Bain, BCG, Catalyst, Deloitte, McKinsey, Mercer, PwC and Women Corporate Directors.

And last, but certainly not least, the Think Glink Media team, without whom we literally would not have gotten this done, especially Ilyce Glink and Kris Mackenzie.

ENDNOTES

[1] Ethier, Marc. "MBA Programs With The Most Women." Poets&Quants. February 24, 2018. Accessed April 30, 2018. https://poetsandquants.com/2018/01/31/which-mba-programs-enroll-the-most-women.

[2] Stahl, Lesley. "Leading by Example to Close the Gender Pay Gap." CBS News. April 15, 2018. Accessed April 30, 2018. https://www.cbsnews.com/news/salesforce-ceo-marc-benioff-leading-by-example-to-close-the-gender-pay-gap/.

[3] "The Class of 2017." Economic Policy Institute. Accessed April 30, 2018. https://www.epi.org/publication/the-class-of-2017.

[4] "Application Trends Survey Report." Accessed April 30, 2018. https://www.gmac.com/market-intelligence-and-research/research-insights.aspx.

[5] Waller, Nikki. "How Men and Women See the Workplace Differently." The Wall Street Journal. August 15, 2016. Accessed April 30, 2018. http://graphics.wsj.com/how-men-and-women-see-the-workplace-differently/.

[6] Luce, Sylvia Ann Hewlett and Carolyn Buck. "Off-Ramps and On-Ramps: Keeping Talented Women on the Road to Success." Harvard Business Review. August 01, 2014. Accessed April 30, 2018. https://hbr.org/2005/03/off-ramps-and-on-ramps-keeping-talented-women-on-the-road-to-success.

[7] Toossi, Mitra. "A Century of Change: The U.S. Labor Force, 1950–2050." Monthly Labor Review, May 2002. https://www.bls.gov/opub/mlr/2002/05/art2full.pdf.

[8] Blount, Sally. "Prioritize Pivot Points: Getting More Women into the C-suite Means Keeping Them in the Talent Pipeline." Quartz Media, July 8, 2017. https://qz.com/1024078/getting-more-women-into-the-c-suite-means-keeping-them-in-the-talent-pipeline/.

[9] Luce, Sylvia Ann Hewlett and Carolyn Buck. "Off-Ramps and On-Ramps: Keeping Talented Women on the Road to Success." Harvard Business Review. August 01, 2014. Accessed April 30, 2018. https://hbr.org/2005/03/off-ramps-and-on-ramps-keeping-talented-women-on-the-road-to-success.

[10] Byker, Tanya. "The Opt-Out Continuation: Education, Work, and Motherhood from 1984 to 2012." The Russell Sage Foundation Journal of the Social Sciences 2, no. 4 (August 29, 2016). August 29, 2016. Accessed June 4, 2018. https://www.rsfjournal.org/doi/full/10.7758/RSF.2016.2.4.02.

[11] Goldin, Claudia, and Lawrence F. Katz. The Career Cost of Family. Report. Department of Economics, Harvard University. 2010. Accessed June 4, 2018. http://workplaceflexibility.org/images/uploads/program_papers/goldin_-_the_career_cost_of_family.pdf.

[12] Hersch, Joni. "Opting out among Women with Elite Education." Accessed June 3, 2018. Https://law.vanderbilt.edu/phd/faculty/joni-hersch/2013_Hersch_Opting_Out_among_Women_with_Elite_Education_REHO.pdf. June 6, 2013.

[13] Researchers looked at University of Chicago Booth School of Business graduates.

[14] Bertrand, Marianne, Claudia Goldin, and Lawerence F. Katz. *Dynamics of the Gender Gap For Young Professionals In the Corporate and Financial Sectors*. Working paper. Cambridge, MA: National Bureau of Economic Research, 2009.

[15] Ortiz-Ospina, Esteban, and Sandra Tzvetkova. "Working Women: Key Facts and Trends in Female Labor Force Participation." Our World in Data. October 16, 2017. Accessed June 04, 2018. https://ourworldindata.org/female-labor-force-participation-key-facts.

[16] Rynes, Sarah L., Barry Gerhart, and Kathleen A. Minette. "The Importance Of Pay In Employee Motivation: Discrepancies Between What People Say And What They Do." *Human Resource Management*43, no. 4 (Winter 2004): 381-94. http://www.utm.edu/staff/mikem/documents/Payasamotivator.pdf.

[17] "War of Words." The Economist. July 14, 2016. Accessed April 30, 2018. https://www.economist.com/news/books-and-arts/21702161-women-are-judged-way-they-speak-war-words.

[18] "'Motherhood Penalty' Can Affect Women Who Never Even Have a Child." NBCNews.com. April 11, 2016. Accessed June 04, 2018. https://www.nbcnews.com/better/careers/motherhood-penalty-can-affect-women-who-never-even-have-child-n548511.

[19] "Raising Kids and Running a Household: How Working Parents Share the Load." Pew Research Center's Social & Demographic Trends Project. November 04, 2015. Accessed June 04, 2018. http://www.pewsocialtrends.org/2015/11/04/raising-kids-and-running-a-household-how-working-parents-share-the-load/.

[20] Luce, Sylvia Ann Hewlett and Carolyn Buck. "Off-Ramps and On-Ramps: Keeping Talented Women on the Road to Success." Harvard Business Review. August 01, 2014. Accessed April 30, 2018. https://hbr.org/2005/03/off-ramps-and-on-ramps-keeping-talented-women-on-the-road-to-success. Luce, Sylvia Ann Hewlett and Carolyn Buck. "Off-Ramps and On-Ramps: Keeping Talented Women on the Road to Success." Harvard Business Review. August 01, 2014. Accessed April 30, 2018. https://hbr.org/2005/03/off-ramps-and-on-ramps-keeping-talented-women-on-the-road-to-success.

[21] Michael Madowitz, Alex Rowell, and Katie Hamm. "Calculating the Hidden Cost of Interrupting a Career for Child Care." Center for American Progress. June 21, 2016. Accessed June 4, 2018. https://www.americanprogress.org/issues/early-childhood/reports/2016/06/21/139731/calculating-the-hidden-cost-of-interrupting-a-career-for-child-care/.

[22] Miller, Claire Cain. "The 10-Year Baby Window That Is the Key to the Women's Pay Gap." The New York Times. April 11, 2018. Accessed April 30, 2018. http://www.nytimes.com/2018/04/09/upshot/the-10-year-baby-window-that-is-the-key-to-the-womens-pay-gap.html?rref=collection/sectioncollection/upshot&action=click&contentCollection=upshot®ion=rank&module=package&version=highlights&contentPlacement=3&pgtype=sectionfront.

[23] "Women and Caregiving: Facts and Figures." Selected Long-Term Care Statistics | Family Caregiver Alliance. December 31, 2003. Accessed June 04, 2018. https://www.caregiver.org/women-and-caregiving-facts-and-figures.

[24] "The MetLife Juggling Act Study." Accessed June 3, 2018. http://www.caregiving.org/data/jugglingstudy.pdf. 1999.

[25] Brown, Jennifer Erin, M.S., J.D., LL.M., Nari Rhee, Ph.D., Joelle Saad-Lessler, Phh.D., and Diane Oakley, M.B.A. *Shortchanged in Retirement: Continuing Challenges to Women's Financial Future*. Report. March 2016. Accessed June 4, 2018. http://laborcenter.berkeley.edu/pdf/2016/NIRS-Women-In-Retirement.pdf.

[26] "The MetLife Study of Caregiving Costs to Working Caregivers: Double Jeopardy for Baby Boomers Caring for Their Parents." Family Caregiver Alliance National Center on Caregiving. 2011. Accessed June 4, 2018. https://www.caregiver.org/45-facts-family-caregivers-research-2011.

[27] Luce, Sylvia Ann Hewlett and Carolyn Buck. "Off-Ramps and On-Ramps: Keeping Talented Women on the Road to Success." Harvard Business Review. August 01, 2014. Accessed April 30, 2018. https://hbr.org/2005/03/off-ramps-and-on-ramps-keeping-talented-women-on-the-road-to-success.

[28] "Having a Working Mother Is Good For You." Having a Working Mother Is Good For You – News – Harvard Business School. May 18, 2015. Accessed April 30, 2018. https://www.hbs.edu/news/releases/Pages/having-working-mother.aspx.

[29] Cast, Carter. *The Right – and Wrong – Stuff: How Brilliant Careers Are Made and Unmade*. New York: PublicAffairs, 2018.

[30] Small, Linda Babcock, Sara Laschever, Michele Gelf, and Deborah Small. "Nice Girls Don't Ask." Harvard Business Review. August 01, 2014. Accessed April 30, 2018. https://hbr.org/2003/10/nice-girls-dont-ask.

[31] Ammerman, Robin J., Pamela Ely, Colleen Stone, Herminia Ibarra, Robin Ely, Deborah Kolb, Boris Groysberg, and Robin Abrahams. "Rethink What You "Know" About High-Achieving Women." Harvard Business Review. January 16, 2015. Accessed June 04, 2018. https://hbr.org/2014/12/rethink-what-you-know-about-high-achieving-women.

[32] Ammerman, Robin J., Pamela Ely, Colleen Stone, Herminia Ibarra, Robin Ely, Deborah Kolb, Boris Groysberg, and Robin Abrahams. "Rethink What You "Know" About High-Achieving Women." Harvard Business Review. January 16, 2015. Accessed June 04, 2018. https://hbr.org/2014/12/rethink-what-you-know-about-high-achieving-women.

[33] Krivkovich, Alexis, Kelsey Robinson, Irina Starikova, Rachel Valentino, and Lareina Yee. "Women in the Workplace 2017." McKinsey & Company. October 2017. Accessed June 04, 2018. https://www.mckinsey.com/global-themes/gender-equality/women-in-the-workplace-2017.

[34] "Leaders & Daughters Global Survey." 2017. Accessed April 30, 2018. https://s3-eu-west-1.amazonaws.com/public-gbda/Leaders_Daughters_Final.pdf.

[35] The Korn Ferry study was supported by a grant from The Rockefeller Foundation as part of its "100x25" initiative, which aims to support the hiring of 100 Fortune 500 women CEOs by 2025.

[36] "Women CEOs Speak: Strategies for the next Generation of Female Executives and How Companies Can Pave the Road." Korn Ferry | Women CEOs Speak. Accessed April 30, 2018. https://engage.kornferry.com/womenceosspeak?_ga=2.241125507.1644453984.1512309537-1918154691.1512309537.

[37] Krivkovich, Alexis, Kelsey Robinson, Irina Starikova, Rachel Valentino, and Lareina Yee. "Women in the Workplace 2017." McKinsey & Company. October 2017. Accessed June 04, 2018. https://www.mckinsey.com/global-themes/gender-equality/women-in-the-workplace-2017.

[38] Leroy, Sophie. "Why Is It so Hard to Do My Work? The Challenge of Attention Residue When Switching between Work Tasks." Organizational Behavior and Human Decision Processes. May 23, 2009. Accessed April 30, 2018. https://www.sciencedirect.com/science/article/pii/S0749597809000399.

[39] This data was compiled from Forbes Fortune 500 lists between 2017 and 2007.

INDEX